Tyranny
Table Manners
& Tiramisu

Also from EATMS Productions

Books on power, survival, women's autonomy, and the systems shaping modern America.

Nonfiction

Billionaires, Capitalism, and Power

Evil and the Mountain Ungreed
Self Help for American Billionaires
Selfish Steve and the Ivory Tower
Tariffs, Taxes, & Face-Eating Leopards
Ban Billionaires: Fascism Fix

Fascism, Religion, and Cultural Control

Self Help for the Manosphere
Fascism 2025
Fascism & the Perverts & the Greed Virus
Christian Fascism Marriage Book
Tyranny, Table Manners, & Tiramisu

Guides for Women's Autonomy and Protection

How to Survive in Post-America as a Woman
Project 2025 American Drag
4B – Burn, Ban, Boycott, Build
4B OG – So No Go GYN
I'm Glad He's Dead

Analysis of Authoritarian Project 2025

Project 2025: The Blueprint
Project 2025: The List
Project 2025, Christian Dumb Dumbs, & The Republican Agenda
Fascism, Project 2025, & The Pinkprint

Modern Rewrites for Women

Stoic Principles Reimagined
Siddhartha Reimagined
The Prince Reimagined for Women
The Art of War Reimagined for Women
The Jungle Reimagined
The Constitution Reimagined for Women

Machine Learning Series

AI, Bitcoin, Nostr for Women
AI, Safety, & Security for Women
AI, Anxiety, & Health for Women
AI, Kids, & Family Safety for Women
AI, Creativity, & Personal Expression for Women
AI, Independent Work, & Parallel Power for Women

Social Systems Series

Emotional Labor for Women
Household Power for Women
Workplace Power for Women
Medical Bias for Women
Aging Systems for Women
Recovery Systems for Women

Fiction

Dystopian Stories of Resistance and Collapse

Propaganda Paige & the Missing Prosperity
Propaganda Paige & the TIDE Manifesto
Propaganda Paige & the Shadow Cartographers
Propaganda Paige & the Prosperity Alliance
Propaganda Paige & the Shattered Truth
Propaganda Paige & the Rising TIDE
Propaganda Paige & the Last Bastion
Propaganda Paige & the Dawn of Prosperity
Project 2025: Dorian — The Last Men
Project 2025: Boy — A Last Men Novel

Tyranny, Table Manners, & Tiramisu:
Winter Cookbook of the Morally Disabled

Braise the Rich 1

by
Flint Ramones

EATMS
PRODUCTIONS

Copyright © 2025 Eatms Productions
All rights reserved.

This title is part of an ongoing body of work. All EATMS Productions titles, across all series, authors, and formats, are components of a single connected project.

No part of this book may be reproduced, or stored in a retrieval system, or transmitted in any form or by any means, electronic, mechanical, photocopying, recording, or otherwise, without express permission in writing from the publisher.

This book is a work of opinion and creative interpretation. While some names and events may be referenced or alluded to, any claims made are based on publicly available information and are intended as satire, parody, or commentary on societal and political issues. The content should not be interpreted as factual assertions about any individual or entity. The author does not intend to defraud, defame, or mislead, and encourages readers to form their own conclusions. Any resemblance to real persons, living or dead, is purely coincidental unless explicitly noted otherwise.

ISBN: 978-1-966014-16-4

Cover, interior design, interior prints by: Esme Mees

eatms@pm.me
www.eatms.me

Printed in the United States of America.

When the people shall have nothing more to eat,
they will eat the rich

— Jean-Jacques Rousseau

Table of Contents

Introduction—Setting the Table for Tyranny　9

Table Manners—Fork It　13

Section 1—Appetizers of Apathy　35

Section 2—Soups of Systemic Failure　47

Section 3—Salads of Scapegoating　59

Section 4—Main Course of Misery　71

Section 5—Desserts of Despair　87

Bonus Section— Entertaining at the End of Empathy　103

Bonus Bonus—Feast for a Crowd　115

A Recipe, or 3, for Prosperity　125

List of Prints　133

About EATMS Productions　135

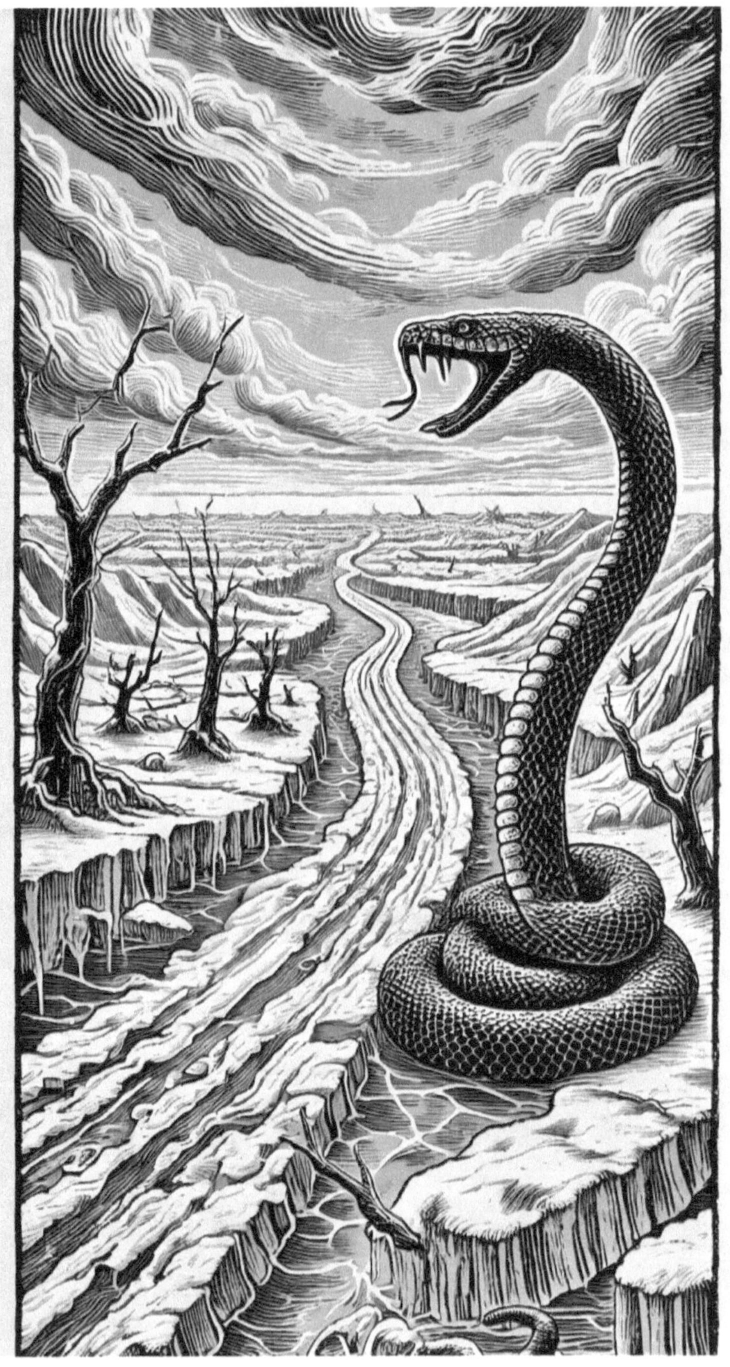

8

Introduction
Setting the Table for Tyranny

Winter, once a season of shared hardship, has become a stark, frozen testament to the failures of unchecked capitalism. The bitter cold is no longer the primary threat to survival, it is the manufactured scarcity, the engineered economic precarity, the deliberate siphoning of resources from the many to the few. While families ration heat, stretch groceries, and work multiple jobs to barely scrape by, the wealthiest among us sit insulated in their climate-controlled mansions, their wealth compounding even in a so-called crisis. The suffering of the working class is not incidental; it is the business model. It is the end result of policies crafted not to serve the people, but to serve the interests of the powerful, ensuring that prosperity is locked away behind iron gates while the rest of us fight for scraps.

They have privatized survival itself. They have turned housing into an asset class instead of a human right, forcing millions into homelessness or rent burdens so high they cannot afford basic necessities. They have transformed healthcare into a luxury, where a single accident or illness can bankrupt a family. They have made education an investment gamble, indebting generations before they ever earn a paycheck. They have taken every tool meant to lift people out of poverty, social programs, public education, labor protections, and either gutted them or sold them off to the highest bidder. And at every turn, they demand that we remain polite about it. They clutch their pearls at anger, at defiance, at any refusal to simply accept the system they have built to serve them and oppress everyone else. They weaponize civility, insisting that it is rude to point out their theft, that it is class warfare to demand fairness, that it is "divisive" to call out injustice.

But winter is also a time of reckoning, a season that reveals who is truly prepared for hardship and who is merely coasting on stolen abundance. The rich have convinced themselves they are untouchable, that their wealth and power will insulate them forever. They believe they will always control the table, that we will always beg for a seat, that we will always obey the rules they set. But they forget that hunger breeds action. They forget that the starving will eat whatever is available. They forget that history has a way of turning feasts into famines for those who hoard too much. They believe that by stripping away protections, they have built an unshakable system, but in reality, they have made themselves vulnerable. They have created a world where they alone have anything left to take.

We are not merely living through an economic downturn or a policy failure. We are witnessing the deliberate and systematic destruction of democracy, the final act of a decades-long con job where wealth is stolen from the working class and funneled to an oligarchy that produces nothing but suffering. The billionaires who control this country do not fear elections or laws, they own both. They do not fear moral arguments or ethical debates, they have long since abandoned any pretense of conscience. The only thing they fear is losing control of the narrative, losing the illusion of legitimacy, losing the ability to convince people that this is simply the way the world must be.

This is a cookbook, yes, but it is also a manual for survival, for opposition, for reclaiming what has been stolen. It does not abide by their table manners because it does not recognize their authority to set them. This is not a polite request for a fairer system, it is an open flame, a call to season the pot, stir the cauldron, and burn down the house that greed built. If they insist on keeping the banquet all to themselves, let them become the main course.

Because there is no compromise with those who would let others starve while they hoard. There is no negotiation with those who build fortunes on suffering. There is no civility to be found in a system that would let children go hungry while billionaires play with vanity projects in space. The time for asking, for waiting, for hoping that they will grow a conscience is long over. The time for taking back what belongs to all of us has begun. These recipes are not just satire, they are warnings. They expose the greed and corruption that have stolen our future, forcing us to face the reality that this **will** be our fate if we do nothing. The ingredients for justice are here. Do we accept the bitter meal they serve us, or burn the kitchen down and cook something better? Every rigged system, every stolen resource continues because they assume we will swallow it. Either we act now or resign ourselves to eating the scraps of a feast we paid for but were never invited to. The recipes are ready. The only missing ingredient is your rage. Time to cook.

Stay seated, or flip the table.
—*TGC* Flint Ramones, Winter 2025

Do Not
Obey
Braise
yum
the RICH

Table Manners: Fork It

A guide to rejecting the false civility of oppressive systems, breaking free from the table set for us, and refusing to play by rules designed to keep us in our place.

The Etiquette of Control

- Table manners aren't about kindness, they're about power.

- The rules of fine dining mirror the unspoken rules of society:

- who speaks, who serves, who eats first, and who gets nothing.

- Just as silverware placement and seating charts uphold hierarchy at a dinner, political and economic systems do the same on a national scale.

- We are expected to behave, to be polite, to "sit at the table" with those who exploit and harm us, but what if we refuse?

The way a table is set isn't just about function; it's about order, tradition, and most of all, control. At a fine dining table, every utensil has its place, every plate is arranged according to an unspoken set of rules, and every guest has a designated seat that determines their importance. These rules aren't questioned; they're followed without hesitation, because to break them, to use the wrong fork, to speak out of turn, to reach across the table, is to signal that you don't belong. But what if these rules weren't just about a meal? What if they were a reflection of something much larger, much more sinister? Because the truth is, the same unspoken laws that govern a formal dinner are the same ones that shape our society. They dictate who speaks first and who must wait their turn. They determine who gets the best cuts and who is left with scraps. They reinforce power in the hands of those who have always had it while ensuring that those beneath them never dare to reach for more.

Society, like a well-set table, is arranged to maintain hierarchy. The wealthiest sit at the head, closest to the best food, where they are served first and have their needs anticipated before they even lift a finger. Their glasses are always full. Their plates are never empty. The middle class sits further down the table, still able to eat, but with less say in what is served. And at the very end, if they are even at the table at all, are the working class, the poor, the disenfranchised, the people whose job isn't to eat but to serve. They bring the food, refill the glasses, clear the plates, and remain invisible unless they make a mistake. They are expected to smile, to be grateful, to accept whatever crumbs fall their way while those at the top continue their feast without a second thought.

This is the etiquette of control. It is why billionaires expect deference even as they hoard resources. It is why politicians who strip away rights demand "respectful discourse" from those whose lives they are destroying. It is why we are told that real change happens through patience, through waiting our turn, through quiet and measured conversation, while those in power never have to wait for anything. They tell us that we must be civil, that we must be polite, that we must follow the rules. But these rules were never meant to serve us. They exist to ensure that power remains where it has always been, untouched, unchallenged, unbothered.

The demand for politeness is not a call for fairness; it is a tool of suppression. They don't want a conversation; they want compliance. They don't want a debate; they want submission. Civility has never been a requirement for those in power. They lie, they cheat, they manipulate, they exploit. They bend the rules to suit their needs and rewrite them when necessary. Yet they expect those beneath them to always follow the rules, to ask nicely, to wait patiently, to accept injustice with grace and restraint. But why should we? Why should we engage in a game where the outcome is already decided? Why should we abide by the etiquette of a system that is built to exclude us?

There is no reward for obedience. There is no prize for playing by their rules. They tell us to wait for justice, but justice delayed is justice denied. They tell us to work harder for a seat at the table, but the table was never meant for us in the first place. They tell us to be grateful for what we have, but what we have was stolen from us long before we were even born. We do not have to abide by their rules. We do not have to play their game. We do not have to sit quietly while they carve up everything and leave us with nothing.

We have been taught to believe that the only way to get a seat at the table is to play nice, to wait our turn, to prove that we deserve to be there. But that is a lie. The reality is that no amount of waiting, no amount of civility, no amount of playing by their rules will ever grant us access to power. They do not want us there. They never have. They never will. The only choice we have left is to refuse. To stop waiting. To stop asking. To stop accepting the place they have given us. If the table is set against us, then it is time to flip the table. If the meal is poisoned, then it is time to walk away. If the rules exist only to keep us in our place, then it is time to break them. Because table manners aren't about kindness, they're about power. And it is time we took that power back.

Setting the Table: Who Gets What and Why

- Forks on the left, knives on the right, sound familiar? The entire system is set up in advance, and you don't get a say in how it's arranged.

- Fine dining etiquette exists to distinguish the wealthy from everyone else, just like American politics keeps the powerful insulated while forcing the rest of us to play by their rules.

- The expectation is that you quietly accept your place. Instead, flip the table.

The placement of silverware at a formal dinner is not random. Forks on the left, knives on the right. Glasses arranged in a precise line above the plate. Napkin folded just so. These rules are not about necessity; they are about signaling who belongs and who does not. Etiquette is not neutral. It is designed to distinguish, to categorize, to ensure that those who were born into wealth and power can move seamlessly through their world while everyone else stumbles, unsure of what they are supposed to do. It is a performance, a ritual of exclusion, a way of reminding people that there are rules they were never taught, customs they were never invited to learn. And if something as small as placing the wrong fork in the wrong hand can mark someone as an outsider, then imagine how much more deeply the rules of society work to keep people in their place. The dinner table is just a reflection of a larger truth: the system is set up long before you arrive, and you are expected to abide by it without question.

In American politics, the seating chart is already written. The menu is already chosen. The most powerful sit closest to the center, where decisions are made and resources are distributed. They receive the first and best portions, served to

them without effort. Their needs are anticipated before they
even ask. Just beyond them, the upper middle class still gets
service, still benefits from proximity to wealth, though they
must work harder to maintain their place. But further down
the table, things begin to change. The food is picked over,
the wine glasses are empty, the plates are chipped. And at the
very end, if they even have a seat at all, are the workers, the
ones who prepared the meal, who refill the glasses, who clean
up the mess when it is over. They are not expected to eat,
only to serve. And if they do get a plate, it is long after the
best has been taken. They are expected to be grateful for
whatever scraps remain.

This is not an accident. This is not a flaw in the system. This
is the system. It was designed this way from the beginning.
There is no neutral, no fair process where everyone has an
equal chance to move up the table. The rules of the meal,
like the rules of the economy, are set up to keep things
exactly as they are. Those at the top will always be served
first. Those at the bottom will always be expected to serve.
Those in between will be given just enough to keep them
from flipping the table over entirely. Every once in a while,
someone from the back might be allowed to move up a seat
or two, a performance meant to prove that the system is fair,
that hard work is rewarded, that patience and respect for the
process will lead to eventual success. But these exceptions do
not change the reality. They are a carefully controlled
illusion meant to keep the majority in their place.

What happens when you do not accept your place? What
happens when you question why the rules exist at all? The
moment you push back, you are met with hostility. Not just
from those at the top, but from those who have internalized
the system, who believe that fairness means following the
rules no matter how rigged they are. They will tell you that
you should wait your turn, that change comes slowly, that
you should be grateful for what you have. They will say that
disrupting the table is impolite, that it is rude, that it is not

how things are done. Because they know that if enough people refuse to play along, the entire system collapses.

The expectation is that you will accept your place, that you will be content with what you are given, that you will sit quietly while others feast. But you do not have to. The table was not set with you in mind. The meal was never meant to be shared equally. You can follow the rules and hope for a better seat someday, or you can recognize the truth: that the only way to change the system is to stop playing by its rules. The expectation is that you will quietly accept your place. Instead, flip the table.

The Glasses Are Always Full—
But Not for You

- At an elite dinner, different people get different glasses. Champagne flutes for the billionaires, fancy wine goblets for the ruling class, and plastic cups for the workers pouring the drinks.

- The trickle-down lie is built into these settings, you're expected to wait patiently while the rich toast to your suffering.

- Stop waiting for a refill. It's never coming.

At an elite dinner, the glass you are given tells you everything about your place in the world. The billionaires at the head of the table drink from delicate champagne flutes, their glasses never empty, their wealth so vast that refills appear before they even notice a drop missing. The ruling class, those just beneath them in the hierarchy, are handed large, fine-stemmed wine goblets, a bit heavier, a bit less delicate, but still a sign of their comfort, their security, their access. Further down the table, the glasses become smaller, cheaper,
18

less refined. Some are scuffed, some mismatched. The middle class gets glass tumblers, decent but not extravagant, sturdy enough to last a while but meant to be replaced. And at the very end of the table, if they even have a seat at all, the workers are handed plastic cups, the kind that are flimsy, disposable, an afterthought. These are the same people who pour the wine, refill the glasses, clear the empty bottles at the end of the night, but their own cups remain dry. They are not meant to drink. They are meant to serve.

The distribution of wealth works the same way. The ultra-rich do not worry about running out, about how much is left, about whether there will be more tomorrow. They do not consider the cost because the cost does not affect them. The ruling class, those close enough to power to benefit from it, drink freely too, maybe with a little more concern, but still with the security of knowing that they will always be taken care of. But the further down you go, the less there is, the more cautious people become. They sip rather than drink, they ration, they plan. They are told that if they work hard enough, if they wait long enough, if they are patient, their glasses will be filled. They are told that the system is fair, that the wine will make its way to them, that there is plenty for everyone. But it never does. It never will.

This is the lie of trickle-down economics, a system designed to ensure that those at the top never run out while those at the bottom are left to believe that, one day, they too will get their share. They will not. The table is set to keep the rich full and the rest waiting, hoping, struggling for drops of what has already been taken from them. It is not about fairness. It is not about hard work. It is about control. The myth of the empty glass, the idea that if you just wait, if you just follow the rules, if you just work harder, you will be rewarded, is one of the most carefully crafted illusions in history. The billionaires who own everything have no intention of letting any of it reach you. The politicians who protect them have no plan to refill your cup. The corporations that profit from your labor have already factored your desperation into their bottom line.

You can keep waiting, keep hoping, keep believing that someday your glass will be filled. Or you can realize the truth. The people at the top are not just drinking from their own glasses, they are drinking from yours. They are drinking from your wages, your healthcare, your education, your retirement. They are drinking from the future you were promised, from the resources that should have been shared, from the wealth created by generations of labor that never saw its fair share. And when they lift their glasses for another toast, when they celebrate their success, when they pat themselves on the back for all they have built, they do it with what was taken from you.

The expectation is that you will wait your turn, that you will be grateful for whatever you are given, that you will trust the system to work in your favor. But it will not. It never has. You can sit at the table with an empty glass, waiting for something that will never come, or you can take what should have been yours all along. Stop waiting for a refill. It is never coming.

Beyond the Table:
No Is Your New Favorite Word

- You are not required to engage in "civil discourse" with people who want you erased.

- You do not owe patience or respect to those who strip away your rights.

- You can say no to debates that question your humanity.

- No is not rudeness, it is resistance.

No is a sentence. No is a boundary. No is a weapon against those who believe they are entitled to your time, your energy, your compliance. From the moment we are old enough to speak, we are trained to soften our refusals, to explain ourselves, to make excuses for why we do not want to engage, to avoid making anyone uncomfortable. We are told that saying no is impolite, that it is aggressive, that it shuts down dialogue, as though dialogue with those who see you as less than human is a virtue. But no is not rudeness. No is resistance. No is the refusal to be dragged into arguments that are not made in good faith. No is the rejection of debates that were never meant to change minds, only to exhaust and humiliate. No is an act of self-preservation in a world that demands your submission under the guise of civility.

The people who insist you must always be willing to engage in debate are not arguing in good faith. They are not looking for understanding. They are looking for an opening. They want you to defend your right to exist over and over again, to prove your worth, to justify your humanity as if it were ever up for discussion. They want to wear you down, to waste your time, to make you so tired that you finally give in and let them have their way. They want you to meet their condescension with patience, to respond to their cruelty with grace, to let them set the terms of the conversation, to force you into a performance of respectability that only benefits them. They want you to be polite as they strip away your rights, measured as they take away your autonomy, calm as they push forward their agenda of control. They believe that if they demand civility while committing harm, you will be trapped by the expectation of politeness, that you will hesitate, that you will let them speak when they should be shut down.

But you do not have to engage. You do not have to sit at their table and entertain their bad-faith arguments. You do not have to debate your right to exist, to love, to be safe, to have control over your own body. You do not have to explain why you do not deserve to be oppressed, why your rights should not be stripped away, why your safety and dignity should not be subject to the whims of those who see you as expendable. You do not have to provide a well-researched rebuttal every time a bigot disguises their hatred as an "opinion." You can simply say no. No, I will not engage with you. No, I will not justify my existence. No, I will not pretend that we are having the same conversation in good faith. No, I will not give you the time, the energy, or the platform you so desperately crave.

There is power in refusal. There is power in cutting off the oxygen that feeds the fire of fascism, in refusing to let those who seek control dictate the terms of the conversation. They expect you to argue with them because they have already decided the argument is not one they can lose. They expect you to try to change their minds because they know they are not at risk of having their minds changed. They expect you to believe that engagement is progress, when engagement is, for them, nothing more than another way to dominate, to control, to manipulate. They want you to think that saying no makes you the problem. That refusing to humor them makes you closed-minded. That standing your ground makes you extreme. That choosing not to debate is an admission of defeat.

But no is not defeat. No is the only response that makes it clear that their game is over. No forces them to confront the fact that you do not recognize their authority, that their demand for attention and legitimacy will go unanswered. No tells them they are irrelevant. No tells them they are powerless. No tells them that the time for negotiation is over. No tells them they do not get to set the terms of your existence. No is not just rejection. No is opposition. No is a refusal to be complicit. No is a reminder that you are not required to be polite in the face of oppression. No is your new favorite word. Use it.

Stop Smiling at Nazis

- The expectation of politeness is a weapon used against you.

- Smiling at fascists does not make them less dangerous, it makes them comfortable.

- Fascists thrive on normalization, on being invited in under the guise of "just another political view."

- Treat them like what they are: a threat that must be shut down, not accommodated.

The expectation of politeness is one of the greatest weapons of control ever created. It is drilled into us from childhood, reinforced in every social interaction, and used as a leash to keep us docile in the face of oppression. Politeness is not just a social norm, it is a system of compliance. It demands that we suppress our anger, that we bite our tongues, that we make room for those who would do us harm. It is why people are told to be "civil" when their rights are being stripped away. It is why we are expected to engage in "reasonable discussion" with those who see us as less than human. It is why we are told to "hear both sides" even when one side is openly advocating for our erasure. And it is why, even in the face of growing fascism, so many people still believe that the best response is to stay calm, to be polite, to smile and hope that decorum will somehow keep the worst from happening. But that is not how this works. Fascists do not care about your civility. They see your politeness as permission.

Smiling at fascists does not make them less dangerous. It makes them comfortable. It tells them they are welcome, that their views are acceptable, that they are safe to spread their ideology without consequence. Fascists thrive on normalization. They do not begin by marching in the streets or taking over governments. They begin by infiltrating polite society, by framing their extremism as "just another political opinion," by slowly shifting the boundaries of what is considered acceptable discourse. They start by suggesting that maybe we should "debate" whether some people deserve rights. They introduce themselves as "rational skeptics," as people who are simply concerned about the direction of the country, as those who just want to have an "honest conversation" about immigration, or gender, or democracy itself. They do not walk in announcing their end goal. They test the waters, pushing the line just a little further each time, seeing how much they can get away with before anyone pushes back. And when no one does, they move further. They escalate. They grow bolder. And before long, what was once unthinkable has become reality.

They count on your politeness. They count on your discomfort with confrontation. They count on the social expectation that it is rude to call someone a fascist, even when they are openly espousing fascist beliefs. They count on you looking away, on you assuming that someone else will handle it, on you telling yourself that it is not yet bad enough to intervene. They count on your instinct to keep the peace. And they weaponize it against you. Because by the time it becomes undeniable, by the time their words turn into actions, by the time their platform has grown too large to ignore, it is too late. The warning signs were there all along. The danger was clear. But they were smiled at. They were accommodated. They were given space to grow.

You do not have to smile at fascists. You do not have to make them comfortable. You do not have to engage in debate, to treat them like they are worth reasoning with, to offer them respect they will never return. You do not owe them civility. What you owe is a refusal to let them exist unchallenged. What you owe is an unflinching rejection of their ideology, not as an abstract danger, but as a real and immediate threat. What you owe is an unwavering stance that they are not welcome, that they will not be tolerated, that they will not find safety in your presence.

Fascism does not disappear on its own. It is not defeated through kindness. It does not crumble under the weight of a well-articulated argument. It must be shut down. It must be crushed. It must be made so impossible, so untenable, so unwelcome that it cannot take root. That does not happen through politeness. It happens through opposition. Through refusal. Through the absolute rejection of their presence in every space they try to infiltrate.

Cultivate Your Own News – You Are What You Consume

- Corporate media is processed junk food, empty, manipulative, designed to keep you passive.

- Social media is an algorithm, not a truth machine. If you don't control what you take in, someone else will do it for you.

- Learn the difference between critical thinking and getting caught in an outrage cycle designed to exhaust you.

The information you consume shapes your reality. It dictates what you believe is possible, what you think is worth fighting for, and what you assume is inevitable. If you let the wrong people control your media diet, they will keep you weak, passive, and afraid. Corporate media is not designed to inform you; it is designed to keep you from asking the wrong questions. It is processed junk food, engineered to look like sustenance but containing nothing of value. It keeps you entertained, outraged, distracted, or exhausted, but never truly informed. Its purpose is to manufacture consent, to normalize injustice, to convince you that power is too vast to challenge. The billionaires who own the networks and newspapers do not want you thinking critically about how the system works. They do not want you connecting the dots between their wealth and your struggles. They want you tuning in just enough to stay hooked, to stay anxious, to stay dependent on their version of the truth, but never enough to see behind the curtain.

Social media is no better. It masquerades as a platform for truth, for democracy, for resistance, but it is an algorithm first and foremost. It is not built to inform, it is built to manipulate. It does not feed you what is most important; it feeds you what is most engaging. Outrage is engagement. Fear is engagement. Division is engagement. The more extreme the headline, the more infuriating the post, the more people argue in the comments, the more profitable the system becomes. It does not care whether you are learning or whether you are being fed lies, it only cares that you stay glued to the screen. The algorithm does not want you thinking deeply, reading critically, making connections between corporate interests, political corruption, and the erosion of civil rights. It wants you scrolling. It wants you consuming whatever gets the most clicks, whatever keeps you bouncing between shock and exhaustion until you are too numb to act.

You must be intentional about what you consume. You must treat information the way you would treat food, questioning the source, the ingredients, the purpose behind it. Who benefits from this story being told in this way? Who is funding the outlet that is presenting it? Who is being protected, and who is being blamed? The goal is not just to be skeptical. Skepticism alone is not critical thinking, it is just another way to be manipulated if you do not know how to sort truth from noise. The goal is to learn how power operates, how media is shaped, how narratives are built to manufacture your beliefs. Once you see it, you cannot unsee it. And once you recognize it, you can no longer participate in it without understanding the cost.

Do not get caught in the outrage cycle. The machine wants you angry but directionless. It wants you mad at the symptoms, not the cause. It wants you arguing over culture wars while ignoring the class war. It wants you pouring your energy into debates that go nowhere while the same people keep getting richer, keep tightening their grip, keep making the rules. Outrage without action is just another form of pacification. Information without strategy is just another way to keep you spinning your wheels. They want you tired. They want you overwhelmed. They want you consuming media like it is a drug, endlessly refreshing, endlessly seeking, never satisfied, never full.

You do not have to play along. You can choose your sources with care. You can step outside the algorithm. You can seek out independent journalism, investigative reporting, primary sources. You can prioritize depth over speed, context over sensation, history over headlines. You can cultivate a media diet that makes you sharper, not weaker. Because you are what you consume, and if you do not control your intake, someone else will. And they will make sure you stay exactly where they want you, distracted, divided, and too exhausted to fight back.

Make Enemies, Not Friends of Everything Corporate

- Corporations are not your allies. They don't "support causes," they co-opt movements to maintain control.

- Stop celebrating when they post rainbow logos or donate scraps to social causes while funding politicians who gut your rights.

- Their only loyalty is to profit, make them your enemy.

Corporations are not your friends. They do not care about justice, equity, or human rights. They are not allies. They are not on your side. They are profit machines, designed to extract as much wealth as possible while giving as little back as they can get away with. They do not "support" causes, they absorb them, water them down, repackage them as branding opportunities, and use them to sell you the illusion of progress. Every time a corporation slaps a rainbow logo on its products in June, every time it tweets a somber message about justice, every time it issues a vague statement about inclusivity, it is not doing so because it believes in those things. It is doing so because it has calculated that it is more profitable to appear progressive than to be exposed as complicit. And in many cases, it is both. The same companies that drape themselves in the language of equality are funding politicians who strip away human rights. The same brands that profit from feminist messaging are built on the exploitation of underpaid women workers. The same corporations that want you to believe they are fighting climate change are burning the planet to the ground in pursuit of record profits.

Stop falling for the performance. Stop celebrating corporations when they do the bare minimum. Stop believing that their marketing strategies are victories. They are not victories. They are distractions. When a billion-dollar company donates a fraction of a percent of its revenue to a cause while spending exponentially more lobbying against policies that would actually help people, that is not progress. That is theft. That is laundering their reputation through your goodwill. That is convincing you that change is happening when, in reality, everything remains exactly as they want it. They do not want liberation. They want compliance. They want you to see them as allies so that you stop fighting them as enemies. They want you to believe that working "within the system" is the solution because they built the system to serve them, and they will never allow it to work against their interests.

There is no ethical consumption under capitalism. You cannot buy your way to justice. But you can refuse to be complicit in corporate propaganda. You can refuse to celebrate when they dangle representation like a prize while continuing to exploit workers and gut protections for the most vulnerable. You can refuse to let them dictate the terms of progress. And most of all, you can stop letting them off the hook. If a company's public message does not match its financial actions, it is not an ally, it is an enemy. If a corporation profits from suffering, from destruction, from human misery, it is not neutral, it is an enemy. If a business model depends on paying workers poverty wages while executives hoard obscene wealth, it is not broken, it is functioning exactly as designed, and it is your enemy.

Make enemies of everything corporate. Stop giving them space in movements they do not belong to. Stop buying into their rebranding of oppression as progress. Stop letting them turn justice into a marketing gimmick. Their only loyalty is to profit, and that makes them the enemy of everyone who believes in something more.

Do Your Homework – Not Just "Research"

- "Do your own research" has been hijacked by bad-faith actors, twisting real analysis into conspiracy-laden garbage.

- Homework means reading history, understanding systemic oppression, and following the money.

- Research that ignores context, expertise, and historical precedent isn't research, it's propaganda.

- Stop falling for the same traps, they've been used before, and they'll be used again.

"Do your own research" has become the rallying cry of bad-faith actors who have no interest in truth. It is a phrase that once meant critical thinking, curiosity, and intellectual rigor, but has now been hijacked by conspiracy theorists, grifters, and manipulators who weaponize it to undermine expertise and spread misinformation. Real research is not scrolling through YouTube videos or finding an obscure blog that confirms your biases. It is not cherry-picking data to support a conclusion you already believe. It is not falling down an internet rabbit hole where every piece of information is curated to keep you engaged, outraged, and disconnected from reality. Research without context is not research. It is propaganda. And propaganda thrives when people mistake skepticism for intelligence, when they assume that simply rejecting the mainstream means they have found the truth.

Homework is different. Homework is hard. It requires discipline. It demands that you go beyond surface-level explanations, beyond what is convenient, beyond what you want to be true. Homework means reading history, real history, not the sanitized versions taught in school or the revisionist nonsense pushed by reactionary politicians.

Homework means understanding systemic oppression, seeing the patterns, recognizing that the injustices of today are not new but part of a long, deliberate history of power protecting itself. Homework means following the money, tracing who benefits, who profits, who funds the narratives being sold to the public. It is uncomfortable. It does not always give you easy answers. But it does give you the ability to see through the lies, the distortions, the carefully constructed illusions meant to keep you powerless.

The traps are always the same. Every time history repeats itself, the justification shifts, the language evolves, but the tactics remain unchanged. Fear, division, scapegoating, manufactured crises, these tools have been used for centuries to keep people from focusing on the real enemy. Economic collapse? Blame the poor, not the billionaires who engineered it. Social unrest? Blame activists, not the systems that created the suffering in the first place. Misinformation spreads because it is easier to believe a simple lie than to confront a complex reality. It is easier to blame a shadowy conspiracy than to accept that capitalism is working exactly as intended. It is easier to believe in villains than to recognize the slow, grinding machinery of greed and power that benefits from your confusion.

You are not immune to propaganda just because you think you are skeptical. You are not automatically informed just because you distrust authority. True critical thinking requires effort, depth, and a willingness to be wrong. It requires questioning not just the mainstream narrative but also the alternatives being sold as radical truth. Because some of them are just another form of control. If you want to understand the world, do your homework. Not just research. Not just soundbites. Not just social media threads. Homework. Because the fight against oppression does not start with outrage. It starts with knowing exactly what you are up against.

Use Their Tools Against Them –
Then Break the Table

- The system expects you to play by its rules, but those rules were written to keep you powerless.

- Learn the strategies of the powerful, then turn them against them.

- Stop asking for a seat at their table, burn the whole thing down and build something better.

The system was never designed for you to win. Every rule, every institution, every so-called neutral process exists to reinforce power where it has always been. They tell you to work within the system, to be patient, to use the channels available to you, but those channels are dead ends, designed to waste your time while they continue hoarding wealth, influence, and control. The people who benefit most from the status quo expect you to follow the rules they wrote, to respect institutions that have never served you, to play a game that was rigged before you were even born. But what happens when you stop playing?

The powerful use their tools to maintain control, but tools are not inherently good or bad, they are just instruments of power. They use the law, media, technology, and economic systems to protect their wealth and limit your ability to fight back. Learn how those tools work. Learn how to disrupt them. Use their tactics against them, undermine their grip, expose their weaknesses. And then, when you've taken everything you can from them, break the table itself. Stop asking for a seat. Stop playing by their rules. The system will never willingly hand over power. It must be dismantled, piece by piece, until something new, something just, is built in its place.

Final Thought:
Starve the Beasts – Starve the Systems

- When we starve fascists, billionaires, and corporate-backed politicians of legitimacy, we make them irrelevant.

- Let them wither. Let them rot. Let them have nothing.

Power does not sustain itself, it feeds on obedience, attention, and the illusion of legitimacy. Fascists, billionaires, and corporate-backed politicians do not hold power because they are inherently stronger or more capable. They hold power because people continue to engage with them, argue with them, acknowledge their authority, and play by their rules. They rely on the belief that they are inevitable, that their control is unshakable, that there is no alternative. But power withers when it is denied the things it feeds on. When billionaires are stripped of their godlike status, when fascists are treated as the pariahs they are instead of just another political perspective, when corporate overlords can no longer buy the loyalty of the masses, they shrink. They lose influence. They rot from within. The only way to win against them is to make them irrelevant, to refuse them the fuel they need to sustain their control.

The systems they built are fragile. They require your labor, your consent, your fear. Starve them of all three. Do not beg for scraps at their table. Do not waste your energy on debates designed to exhaust you. Do not elevate them by treating them as anything more than parasites clinging to a crumbling empire. Let them wither. Let them rot. Let them have nothing. These are the new manners of tyranny, denial, refusal, rejection. The power they hold is only as real as we allow it to be. So stop feeding it.

REFORM

Section 1: Appetizers of Apathy

Appetizers are meant to spark joy, but in the hands of tyranny, they offer only the illusion of comfort. These winter starters are hot on the surface but leave you cold inside.

Recipes:

Healthcare Hummus

Thoughts and Prayers Poppers

Denial Dip

Polar Vortex Veggie Fritters

Seasonal Spineless Wings

There was a time when even the wealthiest understood that they had to throw a few scraps to the working class to prevent outright rebellion. FDR's New Deal, LBJ's Great Society, these were not benevolent gifts from the ruling class, but calculated compromises to keep the working class from revolting. But in the modern era, the billionaires have decided they don't need to pretend anymore. They have stripped away the scraps, leaving behind the illusion of choice, the performative policy gestures, the empty platitudes that amount to nothing. Thoughts and prayers instead of gun control. Market-based solutions instead of universal healthcare. "Both sides" nonsense instead of actual accountability. These appetizers are designed to give the appearance of generosity while offering nothing of real substance, just like the neoliberal policies that keep power in the hands of the few while the rest of us fight over crumbs.

Healthcare Hummus

A Bitter Spread of Overprocessed Bureaucracy and Crushed Public Trust

Serves: The lucky few who can afford it
Prep Time: Endless hold times with insurance
Cook Time: Decades of legislative inaction

Ingredients:

- 2 cups canned chickpeas, drained (because fresh ingredients, like universal healthcare, are unavailable to most)

- ¼ cup privatized tahini (processed through multiple intermediaries, each taking a cut)

- 3 tablespoons lemon juice (squeezed from the crushed hopes of reformers)

- 2 tablespoons olive oil (imported from an industry propped up by subsidies while basic healthcare is gutted)

- 2 cloves garlic (pre-existing condition warning: may increase out-of-pocket costs)

- 1 teaspoon salt (not covered under most plans)

- ½ teaspoon ground cumin (because if you want any flavor, you'll have to pay extra)

- ¼ teaspoon red pepper flakes (representing the fiery rage of every American stuck in medical debt)

- ¼ cup cold water (to thin out your expectations)

Garnish:

- A sprinkle of paprika (cosmetic reform efforts that do nothing to address the real issue)

- A drizzle of olive oil (priced at premium rates for those without employer-sponsored coverage)

- Toasted pine nuts (only available to CEOs of private insurance companies)

Instructions:

1.   **Navigate the Bureaucracy:** Before you even start, take a number and wait indefinitely. Spend some time on hold with customer service while they transfer you between departments. By the time you get through, you will have aged out of your parent's health plan.

2.   **Blend the Base:** In a food processor, combine chickpeas, tahini, lemon juice, olive oil, garlic, salt, and cumin. Pulse until thick and grainy, much like the state of our public healthcare system.

3.   **Thin with False Promises:** Slowly add cold water, one tablespoon at a time, blending until smoother. No matter how much you add, it will never be as smooth as it should be, just like a healthcare system riddled with red tape and profit-driven inefficiency.

4.   **Season with Desperation:** Taste and adjust seasoning. If it feels like it's still missing something, like universal healthcare, affordable prescriptions, or actual patient-first policies, it's because it is.

5.   **Garnish and Serve:** Transfer to a serving dish. Drizzle with olive oil, sprinkle with paprika, and top with pine nuts, unless your deductible doesn't cover it. Serve with stale pita chips, much like the broken promises of affordable coverage.

Serving Suggestions:

•   Pairs well with a side of **Rationed Insulin Pita** or **Prior Authorization Poppers**.

•   Best enjoyed while listening to a politician promise to "study" the issue while cashing checks from the pharmaceutical lobby.

•   May cause unexpected bills months after consumption.

Warning:
This dish is not for those who believe healthcare is a right. Side effects include bankruptcy, rationing medication, lost faith in democracy, and rage at the insurance industry. If symptoms occur, don't call your doctor, you probably can't afford it.

Thoughts and Prayers Poppers

Crispy on the outside, completely hollow inside, just like every politician's response to mass shootings.

Serves: An entire grieving nation, but satisfies no one
Prep Time: However long it takes for lawmakers to send a recycled condolences tweet
Cook Time: Until the next tragedy resets the cycle

Ingredients:

- 10 mini bell peppers (bright and attention-grabbing but empty of substance)

- 4 oz cream cheese (soft and comforting, much like a politician's carefully scripted statement)

- ½ cup shredded cheddar (aged, like the same tired excuses used after every tragedy)

- 2 tablespoons sour cream (for that bitter aftertaste of inaction)

- ½ teaspoon garlic powder (to cover up the stench of corruption)

- ½ teaspoon smoked paprika (a little heat, but not enough to make a difference)

- ¼ teaspoon salt (the tears of grieving families)

- ¼ teaspoon black pepper (like public outrage, brief but ignored)

- 1 cup crushed crackers or panko breadcrumbs (symbolizing shattered trust in our leaders)

- 2 tablespoons melted butter (greasy, just like NRA lobbying money)

Instructions:

1. **Preheat the Distraction:** Set your oven to 375°F, the perfect temperature for warming up empty platitudes.

2.   **Prepare the Poppers:** Cut the tops off each mini bell pepper and scoop out the insides, leaving them completely hollow, just like every "thoughts and prayers" statement.

3.   **Mix the Filling:** In a bowl, combine cream cheese, cheddar, sour cream, garlic powder, paprika, salt, and black pepper. Stir well until blended, just like politicians reheating the same excuses after every mass shooting.

4.   **Stuff with False Hope:** Fill each pepper with the cheese mixture, ensuring it looks substantial at first glance, but ultimately fails to provide anything meaningful.

5.   **Roll in Breadcrumbs:** Coat each stuffed pepper with crushed crackers or panko, sealing in the illusion of action. Brush lightly with melted butter to ensure a glossy, camera-ready appearance.

6.   **Bake Until Forgotten:** Arrange on a baking sheet and bake for 15-18 minutes, or until golden brown, about the same amount of time it takes for public outrage to be dismissed as "too emotional."

7.   **Serve Hot, with a Side of Silence:** Best enjoyed by those who claim the real issue is "mental health" while voting against funding for mental health care.

Serving Suggestions:

- Pairs well with **Gaslighter Gravy**, a sauce designed to shift blame elsewhere.

- Best served at a press conference where politicians insist now is "not the time" for solutions.

- Enjoy with a tall glass of **Filibuster Fizz**, a drink that promises reform but never delivers.

Warning:
May cause frustration, loss of faith in government, and uncontrollable rage. Side effects include endless cycles of inaction, rising gun deaths, and politicians sending prayers instead of passing laws. If symptoms persist, demand actual change, but don't expect results.

Denial Dip

A smooth, cheesy blend of willful ignorance and empty promises, best served with a side of gaslighting. Melts quickly under pressure.

Serves: The uninformed masses, while the rich double-dip into corporate tax breaks
Prep Time: Decades of deregulation and distraction
Cook Time: As long as it takes for reality to set in

Ingredients:

- 8 oz cream cheese, softened (thick and processed, like every politician's excuse)

- 1 cup shredded cheddar (aged, much like outdated economic theories)

- ½ cup sour cream (bitter, like the realization that nothing will change)

- 1 teaspoon garlic powder (to mask the stench of corruption)

- ½ teaspoon smoked paprika (adds drama without real substance)

- ½ teaspoon salt (not enough to fix anything)

- ¼ teaspoon cayenne pepper (a flash of heat, quickly ignored)

- ½ cup crumbled bacon (distracts from the lack of real solutions)

Instructions:

1. **Preheat the Distraction:** Set your oven to 375°F, the same temperature at which lawmakers pretend to care.

2. **Blend the Excuses:** In a mixing bowl, combine cream cheese, cheddar, sour cream, garlic powder, paprika, salt, and cayenne. Stir until smooth, like every well-rehearsed lie about why things can't change.

3. **Top with Diversion:** Sprinkle crumbled bacon on top. Much like corporate media coverage, this adds flavor but does nothing to address the real issue.

40

4.   **Bake Until Forgotten:** Transfer to a small baking dish and heat for 15 minutes, or until bubbly, roughly the time it takes for a scandal to be buried under the next distraction.

5.   **Serve Hot, But Not Too Hot:** Let cool slightly before serving. The last thing we want is for people to get burned by the truth.

Serving Suggestions:

•   Best enjoyed at a corporate fundraiser where billionaires claim poverty is a personal failure.

•   Pairs well with **Whataboutism Crackers**, designed to shift blame in every bite.

•   Serve with a tall glass of **Crisis Chardonnay**, a wine aged in deflection and denial.

Warning:
Side effects include misinformation, manufactured outrage, and the inability to recognize systemic issues. If you experience critical thinking, stop consuming immediately and consult a lobbyist.

Polar Vortex Veggie Fritters

Lightly crisped on the outside, frozen solid in the middle, just like government action on climate change. Fried in oil subsidized by taxpayers, ensuring the problem only gets worse.

Serves: Billionaires who will flee to luxury bunkers, while the rest of us weather the storm
Prep Time: Decades of ignoring climate scientists
Cook Time: Until the last glacier melts

Ingredients:

- 2 cups shredded zucchini and carrots (because fresh produce is getting harder to afford)

- ½ cup frozen corn (much like meaningful climate legislation, cold, but barely holding on)

- ½ cup finely diced onion (representing the tears shed over environmental collapse)

- ½ cup all-purpose flour (binding together false hopes and corporate greenwashing)

- 2 eggs, beaten (as fragile as our infrastructure)

- ½ teaspoon garlic powder (to mask the stench of inaction)

- ½ teaspoon smoked paprika (a little heat, but not enough to change the forecast)

- ½ teaspoon salt (a small taste of what's left of our natural resources)

- ¼ teaspoon black pepper (as effective as a "carbon offset" in fixing the real problem)

- ½ teaspoon baking powder (to create the illusion of rising progress)

- ½ cup oil for frying (preferably something fossil-fuel based, in keeping with tradition)

Instructions:

1.   **Prepare the Frozen Reality:** Toss shredded zucchini and carrots with salt and let sit for 10 minutes, then squeeze out excess water, because nothing will drain faster than government funding for clean energy.

2.   **Mix the Climate Denial Batter:** In a large bowl, whisk together flour, eggs, garlic powder, paprika, black pepper, and baking powder. Stir in the drained veggies and frozen corn, ensuring an uneven consistency, much like global climate policy.

3.   **Heat the Fossil Fuels:** In a heavy skillet, heat oil over medium heat. Just like Big Oil's profits, make sure it's sizzling hot.

4.   **Fry Until We're Doomed:** Scoop small portions into the pan, flatten slightly, and fry for 3 minutes per side, or until golden brown, much like the last rainforest before deforestation claims it.

5.   **Serve Hot, Before the World Burns:** Transfer to a paper towel-lined plate, blotting excess oil, though much like corporate climate pledges, the damage is already done.

Serving Suggestions:

•   Best enjoyed during a winter heatwave while billionaires vacation in space.

•   Pairs well with **Deregulation Ranch Dip**, a creamy sauce that does nothing to stop the burn.

•   Serve with a **Melted Ice Cap Mojito**, a chilling reminder that some things won't come back.

Warning:
Side effects include increased natural disasters, skyrocketing insurance rates, and billionaires telling you to "just move" when your home floods. If symptoms persist, consider overthrowing fossil fuel interests, but don't expect Congress to help.

Seasonal Spineless Wings

Boneless, gutless, and lacking any real substance, just like politicians who refuse to stand up to corporate greed. Lightly seasoned with bipartisan cowardice and fried until all accountability disappears.

Serves: A room full of lawmakers too afraid to take a stand
Prep Time: However long it takes for a bill to die in committee
Cook Time: Just enough to create the illusion of action

Ingredients:

- 1 pound boneless chicken bites (because real backbone was removed decades ago)

- ½ cup buttermilk (as weak as the latest corporate "accountability" pledge)

- 1 cup all-purpose flour (to coat everything in meaningless platitudes)

- 1 teaspoon salt (for the tears of those who expected real leadership)

- ½ teaspoon black pepper (a weak attempt at adding some heat)

- ½ teaspoon smoked paprika (for the appearance of boldness without the actual courage)

- ½ teaspoon garlic powder (to cover up the stench of broken promises)

- ½ teaspoon onion powder (because transparency isn't on the menu)

- ½ teaspoon cayenne (not enough to make a real difference)

- 1 cup oil for frying (heavily subsidized, just like fossil fuels and corporate bailouts)

Instructions:

1.   **Marinate in Buttermilk and Indecision:** In a bowl, soak chicken bites in buttermilk, allowing them to absorb the mild, non-threatening flavor of centrist appeasement. Let sit for 20 minutes, or until any remaining backbone has completely dissolved.

2.   **Coat in Platitudes:** In a separate bowl, whisk together flour, salt, pepper, paprika, garlic powder, onion powder, and cayenne. Dredge the chicken in the mixture, ensuring each piece is thoroughly coated in empty rhetoric.

3.   **Fry Until Accountability Disappears:** Heat oil in a large skillet over medium heat. Fry the coated chicken pieces for about 4 minutes per side, or until golden brown, just long enough for lawmakers to move on to their next hollow statement.

4.   **Drain and Serve Lukewarm:** Remove from oil, drain on paper towels, and serve immediately, though they are best enjoyed cold, just like every corporate-driven policy decision.

Serving Suggestions:

•   Pairs well with **Whataboutism Wing Sauce**, a slippery, deflecting glaze that avoids all real responsibility.

•   Serve with **Lobbyist Blue Cheese Dip**, made with just enough corporate cash to make it palatable.

•   Best enjoyed at a fundraising dinner where politicians pretend to care about working people.

Warning:
These wings contain no real substance and may leave you unsatisfied. Side effects include public outrage, a lack of policy change, and billionaires continuing to profit while spineless leaders do nothing. If consumed regularly, expect increased wealth inequality and a complete loss of faith in government.

46

Section 2: Soups of Systemic Failure

Soup is supposed to warm the soul, but these winter bowls are seasoned with systemic failures. Each spoonful reveals how institutions leave the masses out in the cold

Recipes:

Student Debt Split Pea Soup

Prison-Industrial Chowder

Homelessness Hot Pot

Medicare Part F U Soup

Gerrymandered Gumbo

For generations, the American dream was sold as a promise: work hard, follow the rules, and you will be rewarded. But the Supreme Court, packed with corporate lackeys and Federalist Society ghouls, has rewritten the rules to ensure that success is not a matter of effort but of birthright. Billionaires pay less in taxes than their secretaries, Wall Street criminals receive government bailouts while families are evicted, and CEOs are rewarded for gutting pensions and outsourcing jobs. Every major system, education, healthcare, criminal justice, housing, infrastructure, has been intentionally dismantled in service of greed. The people drowning in student debt, dying from rationed insulin, or working three jobs just to afford rent are not suffering because of bad luck; they are suffering by design. These soups reflect the slow boil of systemic failure, the way institutions once meant to serve the public have been hollowed out and sold for parts.

Student Debt Split Pea Soup

A thick, murky soup simmered in broken promises and garnished with garnished wages. Every spoonful is a reminder that higher education in America is just another debt trap.

Serves: A generation drowning in loan payments while billionaires hoard tax breaks
Prep Time: Four years of college, plus a lifetime of financial burden
Cook Time: 30 years, or until forgiveness is denied for the tenth time

Ingredients:

- 2 cups dried split peas (crushed under financial stress, much like today's graduates)

- 1 medium onion, diced (representing the tears shed over student loan statements)

- 2 carrots, chopped (the bright future you were promised but can't afford)

- 2 celery stalks, chopped (because budgeting for food is now optional)

- 3 cloves garlic, minced (for that bitter aftertaste of predatory interest rates)

- 6 cups water or broth (watered-down, just like the idea of affordable education)

- 1 teaspoon salt (not enough to season the bitter reality of debt servitude)

- ½ teaspoon black pepper (for the slim chance of meaningful loan reform)

- ½ teaspoon smoked paprika (symbolizing the smoke-and-mirrors of debt relief programs)

- 1 bay leaf (because every financial expert tells you to "just wait it out")

- 1 cup diced ham or bacon (optional, since most graduates can't afford protein)

48

Instructions:

1. **Sort Through the Debris:** Rinse and pick over split peas, removing any hard pieces, much like a student sorting through predatory loan offers disguised as "financial aid."

2. **Sauté the Desperation:** In a large pot, sauté onions, carrots, celery, and garlic until softened, much like a graduate realizing their degree has left them underpaid and overworked.

3. **Add the False Promises:** Pour in water or broth, then stir in split peas, salt, pepper, paprika, and the bay leaf. Bring to a boil, then reduce heat and let simmer, just like politicians who stall on loan forgiveness while raking in lobbyist donations.

4. **Cook Until There's No Way Out:** Let simmer for 60-90 minutes, stirring occasionally, until the peas break down completely, leaving behind a thick, inescapable financial mess. Remove bay leaf before serving, because waiting for relief only leads to disappointment.

5. **Serve Hot, Alongside a Side Hustle:** Ladle into bowls and top with diced ham or bacon, if you can afford the luxury. Otherwise, just enjoy it plain, like your stripped-down post-graduate lifestyle.

Serving Suggestions:

*   Best paired with **Ramen Noodles of Regret**, the only meal most borrowers can afford.

*   Serve with **Adjunct Professor Toast**, an underpaid, overworked addition that won't last long.

*   Pairs well with **Deferred Payment Tea**, a beverage steeped in delayed disappointment.

Warning:

May cause stress, financial instability, and an urge to scream at your next loan servicer. Side effects include endless interest accumulation, a total lack of homeownership, and the realization that your student loan payments have done nothing to reduce the balance. If symptoms persist, demand actual reform, but don't expect results.

Prison-Industrial Chowder

A thick, heavy soup that traps everything inside, simmered in systemic injustice and over-seasoned with privatized profit. Designed to keep the few well-fed while the many are left behind bars, literally and financially.

Serves: Corporate prison investors, politicians, and anyone profiting off mass incarceration
Prep Time: A lifetime of systemic inequality
Cook Time: Until reform is permanently locked away

Ingredients:

- 2 cups diced potatoes (representing lives sentenced for minor offenses)

- 1 small onion, chopped (for the tears shed by families torn apart)

- 2 cloves garlic, minced (to mask the stench of for-profit punishment)

- 1 cup corn (because the prison labor system still mimics slavery)

- ½ cup diced carrots (shredded, like public defenders with no resources)

- 2 cups vegetable or chicken broth (funding for public services that instead gets funneled into private prisons)

- 1 cup heavy cream (because profit margins must always be thickened)

- 1 cup shredded cheddar (aged, like sentencing laws designed to punish instead of rehabilitate)

- 1 teaspoon salt (symbolizing the over-policing of marginalized communities)

- ½ teaspoon black pepper (as useful as a non-violent offender's parole hearing)

- ½ teaspoon smoked paprika (because everything about this system is cooked)

- 2 tablespoons butter (melting away like public faith in justice)

Instructions:

1. **Sauté the Injustice:** In a large pot, melt butter over medium heat. Add onions, garlic, and carrots, cooking until softened, much like communities subjected to decades of over-policing and mass incarceration.

2. **Simmer the Systemic Corruption:** Stir in potatoes, corn, broth, salt, pepper, and paprika. Bring to a boil, then reduce heat and let simmer until everything is thick and unescapable, like mandatory minimum sentencing.

3. **Add the Cream and Cheese:** Slowly stir in the heavy cream and shredded cheddar, allowing it to melt into the system, just like how prison contracts funnel public funds straight into private pockets.

4. **Serve with a Side of No Second Chances:** Ladle into bowls and top with a sprinkle of additional cheddar, though, much like rehabilitation programs, this step is purely optional.

Serving Suggestions:

- Best enjoyed at a **Bipartisan Crime Bill Banquet**, where leaders agree that locking up more people is good business.

- Pairs well with **Three-Strike Biscuits**, a dish that ensures one mistake ruins everything.

- Serve with a **Cash Bail Spritzer**, a beverage only available to those who can afford it.

Warning:
May cause financial ruin, broken communities, and unchecked corporate greed. Side effects include prison labor exploitation, extreme racial disparities, and a permanent criminal record for the underprivileged, while wealthy offenders walk free. If symptoms persist, don't bother calling for reform; lawmakers already cashed their checks.

Homelessness Hot Pot

A boiling cauldron of bad policy, systemic neglect, and manufactured scarcity. Packed with evictions, unaffordable housing, and the lingering taste of billionaire-backed gentrification. Serves the wealthy well, while leaving millions out in the cold.

Serves: Real estate investors, hedge funds, and politicians who think homelessness is a "personal failure"
Prep Time: Decades of deregulation, wage stagnation, and gutting public housing
Cook Time: Until every city becomes unlivable for the working class

Ingredients:

- 4 cups broth (watered down, like every underfunded public housing program)

- 1 cup thinly sliced mushrooms (for those forced to live in the shadows)

- 1 cup tofu or shredded chicken (symbolizing the instability of gig economy jobs)

- 1 cup cabbage, chopped (because nutrition is a privilege)

- 1 small onion, sliced (for the tears shed over unaffordable rent)

- 2 cloves garlic, minced (to cover up the stench of rising evictions)

- 1 tablespoon soy sauce (aged, like every empty promise to fix the crisis)

- 1 teaspoon chili flakes (a small, fleeting spark of outrage before people move on)

- ½ teaspoon black pepper (as effective as "sweeps" that criminalize poverty)

- 1 block of instant ramen noodles (cheap, like the excuses from city officials)

- ½ cup bean sprouts (representing the resilience of those forced to survive on nothing)

Instructions:

1. **Heat the Indifference:** In a large pot, bring the broth to a simmer. Much like government action on homelessness, it should be weak, ineffective, and stretched too thin to be useful.

2. **Toss in the Systemic Failures:** Add mushrooms, tofu, cabbage, onion, and garlic. Stir occasionally, ensuring that everything gets evenly displaced, just like families when another luxury condo development forces out longtime residents.

3. **Season with Misdirection:** Stir in soy sauce, chili flakes, and black pepper. Let the flavors blend, though, like most proposed solutions, it won't actually fix the problem.

4. **Throw in the Last-Minute "Solutions":** Add instant ramen and bean sprouts, because when all else fails, society expects the homeless to survive on scraps and makeshift meals. Simmer for 5 more minutes, or until everything is barely holding together.

5. **Serve Hot, Preferably in a Tent on the Sidewalk:** Ladle into bowls and distribute unevenly, much like housing assistance that never reaches those who need it most.

Serving Suggestions:

•   Best paired with **Eviction Notice Crackers**, a brittle, flavorless side that crumbles under the slightest pressure.

•   Serve with a **Luxury Developer Spritzer**, a sparkling beverage that raises property values while displacing thousands.

•   Enjoy with **Bootstrap Brew** a bitter, watered-down drink that politicians swear will fix everything, if only you'd work harder.

Warning:
Consumption may lead to increased public outcry, media lip service, and absolutely no policy change. Side effects include skyrocketing rent, increased criminalization of homelessness, and billionaires hoarding empty properties while millions sleep in the cold. If symptoms persist, remember: there is no crisis, only a system functioning exactly as designed.

Medicare Part F U Soup

A thin, privatized broth packed with hidden fees, rising premiums, and the unmistakable aftertaste of corporate greed. Guaranteed to leave you broke before it leaves you full.

Serves: Private insurers, pharmaceutical CEOs, and politicians with government-funded healthcare
Prep Time: A lifetime of payroll taxes, stolen at the last minute
Cook Time: Until every last dollar has been extracted from patients

Ingredients:

- 4 cups hospital broth (watered down, like Medicare benefits after privatization)

- 2 cups shredded medical bills (because you'll be drowning in them anyway)

- 1 cup diced prescription drug price hikes (marked up 500% for no reason)

- ½ cup thinly sliced bureaucratic red tape (adds no nutritional value, but plenty of frustration)

- 1 medium onion, chopped (for the tears shed over denied claims)

- 2 cloves garlic, minced (to ward off for-profit insurance reps)

- ½ teaspoon salt (because you'll have to ration everything, including flavor)

- ½ teaspoon black pepper (for the sting of another rejected procedure)

- ½ teaspoon cayenne (to represent the burning rage of every American stuck on hold with their insurer)

- 1 cup cooked rice or noodles (a filler, since real solutions are unaffordable)

- ½ cup pre-existing condition croutons (warning: may be denied at the last second)

Instructions:

1. **Prepare the Base of Frustration:** In a large pot, heat the hospital broth over medium heat, make sure it's stretched thin to cover as little as possible.

2. **Add the Corporate Markups:** Stir in shredded medical bills, drug price hikes, and red tape, ensuring a thick, uneven consistency, like every attempt to navigate the U.S. healthcare system.

3. **Simmer in Indifference:** Add onion, garlic, salt, and pepper. Let cook until the mixture becomes impossible to untangle, much like Medicare Advantage plans designed to confuse seniors into overpaying.

4. **Toss in the Rationed Ingredients:** Stir in rice or noodles, but not too much, just like actual care, it's limited by cost-cutting measures.

5. **Garnish with Crushed Dreams:** Top with pre-existing condition croutons, though they may disappear before reaching your bowl.

6. **Serve with an Unexpected Bill:** Ladle into bowls, charge $400 for the spoon, and remind diners they should have read the fine print.

Serving Suggestions:

- Best paired with **Deductible Dumplings**, which vanish the moment you need them.

- Serve with a **Pharmaceutical Price-Gouging Breadstick**, marked up beyond affordability.

- Enjoy with **Prior Authorization Punch**, a drink you'll never actually get to consume.

Warning:
May cause bankruptcy, endless paperwork, and severe distrust in the government. Side effects include denied coverage, lifetime medical debt, and politicians insisting that "we just can't afford universal healthcare," while funding another tax cut for billionaires. If symptoms persist, move to a country with actual healthcare.

Gerrymandered Gumbo

A heavily redrawn recipe where some ingredients count more than others, cooked in a broth of corruption and served unevenly to ensure the powerful always get the best bite. No matter how much you stir, the system stays rigged.

Serves: Career politicians, corporate lobbyists, and billionaires who like picking their own voters
Prep Time: Decades of strategic voter suppression
Cook Time: Until democracy is fully diluted

Ingredients:

- 4 cups politically watered-down broth (seasoned to favor incumbents)

- 1 pound sausage, sliced (packed with pork barrel spending)

- 1 cup diced chicken (voters forced to jump through hoops to cast a ballot)

- 1 large onion, chopped (to represent the many layers of corruption)

- 2 cloves garlic, minced (because nothing stinks like district lines drawn in secret)

- 1 cup diced bell peppers (cut and reshaped beyond recognition)

- 1 cup okra, sliced (to thicken the mess that is partisan redistricting)

- 1 can diced tomatoes (the illusion of representation, but mostly filler)

- 2 teaspoons Cajun seasoning (spicy enough to distract from what's really happening)

- 1 teaspoon black pepper (for the voters who still bother to show up)

- ½ teaspoon cayenne (just enough heat to make people mad, but not enough to change anything)

- 1 bay leaf (because every election cycle, they tell us "just wait for next time")

- ½ cup rice (symbolizing voters who are lumped together in "safe" districts)

Instructions:

1. **Rig the Base:** In a large pot, heat the politically watered-down broth over medium heat. Ensure it's seasoned to benefit those already in power.

2. **Sauté the Manipulation:** Cook sausage, chicken, onions, garlic, and bell peppers in a separate pan until they blend together, like party insiders cutting backroom deals to keep their seats.

3. **Combine and Cover with Misdirection:** Transfer the sautéed mix to the pot. Stir in okra and tomatoes, ensuring that everything gets redistributed, but only to benefit those in charge.

4. **Let Simmer Until Hope is Gone:** Add Cajun seasoning, black pepper, cayenne, and bay leaf. Reduce heat and let simmer for as long as it takes for voters to realize their voice doesn't matter.

5. **Serve Over Divided Rice:** Spoon gumbo over rice, making sure some portions are overflowing while others get barely anything, just like how district lines are drawn.

Serving Suggestions:

- Best enjoyed at a **State Legislature Luncheon**, where representatives get to pick their voters, not the other way around.

- Serve with **Voter Suppression Cornbread**, a dish that looks welcoming but is intentionally made difficult to access.

- Pairs well with **Filibuster Fizz**, a drink that drags everything out until nothing meaningful happens.

Warning:
May cause frustration, voter apathy, and distrust in democracy. Side effects include bizarrely shaped districts, one-party rule, and lawmakers serving longer than monarchs. If symptoms persist, demand voting rights protections, but expect them to be ignored.

EQUALITY

Section 3: Salads of Scapegoating

Even in winter, salads can be fresh and invigorating. These, however, are frosty metaphors for scapegoating and the cruelty of systemic oppression

Recipes:

Reproductive Rights Roasted Root Salad

Both Sides Brussels Sprout Salad

Immigration Winter Slaw

Woke Watercress and Citrus Salad

Blame Game Beet and Goat Cheese Salad

When the ruling class fails to deliver, they do not apologize or change course; they redirect the blame. It is never the fault of the billionaires who hoard wealth, or the corporations that ship jobs overseas, or the politicians who serve their donors instead of their constituents. Instead, they blame immigrants, the poor, Black and brown communities, women, LGBTQ+ people, anyone but the actual architects of inequality. The Supreme Court, having already sold democracy to the highest bidder, acts as an enforcement wing for these manufactured crises, gutting reproductive rights, dismantling labor protections, and ensuring that white Christian nationalism remains the dominant power structure. These salads represent the cold, crisp deception of scapegoating, a fresh coat of dressing on a rotten foundation.

Reproductive Rights Roasted Root Salad

A once-balanced dish now stripped of choice ingredients, forcefully modified by lawmakers with no culinary experience. Seasoned with bad faith, overcooked with moral panic, and served cold to those with no say in the recipe.

Serves: Theocrats, forced-birth extremists, and legislators who wouldn't know a uterus from a turnip
Prep Time: Decades of systemic control over women's bodies
Cook Time: Until all autonomy is legislated away

Ingredients:

- 2 large sweet potatoes, diced (for the sweetness of freedom, rapidly disappearing)

- 3 carrots, chopped (representing the generations fighting for rights their mothers had)

- 2 beets, peeled and quartered (the deep red of every unnecessary medical complication caused by abortion bans)

- 1 small red onion, sliced (for the countless tears shed over lost bodily autonomy)

- 2 tablespoons olive oil (to grease the pockets of anti-choice lobbyists)

- 1 teaspoon sea salt (not enough to heal the wounds of forced birth)

- ½ teaspoon black pepper (to mask the bitterness of state-mandated suffering)

- ½ teaspoon smoked paprika (symbolizing the fiery rage of those still fighting back)

- 2 tablespoons apple cider vinegar (for the sour aftertaste of Supreme Court decisions)

- ½ cup crumbled goat cheese (optional, much like contraception under an extremist regime)

- ¼ cup toasted pecans (because every draconian policy is just nuts)

- 1 handful arugula (to add some bite, since lawmakers think women shouldn't have any)

Instructions:

1. **Preheat the Regression:** Set your oven to 400°F, the perfect temperature for baking outdated laws into modern life.

2. **Toss in Control:** In a large bowl, mix sweet potatoes, carrots, beets, and red onion with olive oil, salt, pepper, and smoked paprika. Spread on a baking sheet, ensuring the most vulnerable pieces get burned first.

3. **Roast Until Rights are Unrecognizable:** Bake for 30-35 minutes, flipping halfway through, or until everything is tender, unlike the hearts of those legislating reproductive rights away.

4. **Dress in Bad Faith Arguments:** Whisk together apple cider vinegar and olive oil, then drizzle over the cooled roasted vegetables, ensuring every bite carries a sour note.

5. **Top with Unwanted Opinions:** Toss the roasted vegetables with arugula, goat cheese (if available), and pecans before serving. Much like access to reproductive healthcare, ingredients may vary by state.

Serving Suggestions:

- Best enjoyed at a **Congressional Luncheon on Women's Issues**, where men do all the talking.

- Pairs well with **Comstock Crackers**, dry and tasteless like 19th-century morality laws making a comeback.

- Serve with **Judicial Overreach Dressing**, a sauce that ruins everything it touches.

Warning:
May cause rage, despair, and a strong urge to move to a country with actual reproductive rights. Side effects include maternal mortality, unsafe procedures, and extremists controlling healthcare decisions. If symptoms persist, vote like your life depends on it, because it does.

Both Sides Brussels Sprout Salad

A bitter, overcooked dish desperately trying to appeal to everyone but satisfying no one. Tossed in false equivalencies and served cold, because real accountability is never on the menu.

Serves: Centrist politicians, corporate media pundits, and people who think compromise with fascists is possible
Prep Time: However long it takes to frame oppression as a "difference of opinion"
Cook Time: Just long enough to ensure nothing changes

Ingredients:

- 3 cups Brussels sprouts, halved (because like democracy, they've been divided beyond recognition)

- 2 tablespoons olive oil (greasing the palms of those who pretend to care)

- ½ teaspoon salt (to season the wounds of those forced to "debate" their own humanity)

- ½ teaspoon black pepper (because mild outrage is all the media allows)

- 1 teaspoon honey (a spoonful of sugar to help the both-sides-ism go down)

- 1 tablespoon balsamic vinegar (aged in decades of bad-faith arguments)

- ¼ teaspoon crushed red pepper flakes (for a little heat, but not enough to make a real impact)

- ½ cup crumbled goat cheese (optional, much like moral conviction in Washington)

- ¼ cup toasted walnuts (because this entire approach is just nuts)

Instructions:

1. **Preheat the False Neutrality:** Set your oven to 400°F, the perfect temperature for roasting an issue until it's charred beyond recognition.

2. **Toss in Misdirection:** In a large bowl, mix Brussels sprouts with olive oil, salt, and pepper, ensuring each piece is coated in a thin layer of meaningless moderation.

3. **Bake Until the Middle is Mushy:** Spread Brussels sprouts onto a baking sheet and roast for 20-25 minutes, flipping halfway through, much like politicians who flip their stance when convenient.

4. **Dress with False Balance:** Drizzle with honey and balsamic vinegar, creating a misleadingly sweet and sour combination that ultimately leaves a bad taste.

5. **Finish with a Sprinkle of Cowardice:** Toss in goat cheese and walnuts, because at the last second, someone always tries to make this palatable without actually fixing anything.

Serving Suggestions:

- Best enjoyed at a **Cable News Roundtable**, where serious issues are debated like they're team sports.

- Pairs well with **Whataboutism Dressing**, a tangy, deflective sauce that dodges every real question.

- Serve with **Centrist Croutons**, dry, flavorless, and entirely unnecessary.

Warning:
May cause frustration, regression of civil rights, and the continued normalization of extremism. Side effects include political gridlock, manufactured outrage, and the creeping realization that "both sides" only ever benefits one. If symptoms persist, try standing for something.

Immigration Winter Slaw

A cold, bitter mix of shredded opportunity and razor-thin chances, tossed in political fear-mongering and served with a side of hypocrisy. Designed to be picked apart by those who built their own wealth off the backs of immigrants.

Serves: Corporate employers who rely on underpaid labor while funding anti-immigrant policies
Prep Time: Generations of exploitation, detention, and ever-moving goalposts
Cook Time: Frozen indefinitely in bureaucratic limbo

Ingredients:

- 3 cups shredded cabbage (tough, resilient, and fundamental, like immigrant labor)

- 1 cup julienned carrots (representing the families separated at borders)

- ½ cup thinly sliced red onion (for the layers of legal loopholes designed to keep citizenship out of reach)

- ½ cup dried cranberries (sweet, like the empty promises made during election seasons)

- ¼ cup pumpkin seeds (for those who put down roots, only to be told they don't belong)

- 2 tablespoons olive oil (greasing the system that exploits immigrant labor while demonizing it)

- 1 tablespoon apple cider vinegar (a sour reminder that "the land of opportunity" isn't for everyone)

- 1 teaspoon honey (a small gesture of kindness, overshadowed by systemic cruelty)

- ½ teaspoon salt (the tears of those waiting years for a path to citizenship)

- ½ teaspoon black pepper (for the constant surveillance and policing of immigrant communities)

- ¼ teaspoon crushed red pepper flakes (a sharp kick, much like every racist policy disguised as "security")

Instructions:

1. **Shred the Stability:** In a large bowl, combine cabbage, carrots, and red onion, slicing them as thinly as the chances of ever achieving legal status.

2. **Toss in the Political Contradictions:** Add cranberries and pumpkin seeds, ensuring that contributions are recognized but never properly valued.

3. **Dress in Fear and False Promises:** In a separate bowl, whisk together olive oil, apple cider vinegar, honey, salt, black pepper, and red pepper flakes. Pour over the slaw, coating everything in just enough lip service to keep hope alive.

4. **Chill Until Forgotten:** Refrigerate for at least 30 minutes, much like immigration reform, left to sit indefinitely while lawmakers move on to more profitable distractions.

Serving Suggestions:

•	Best enjoyed at a **Campaign Fundraiser**, where politicians pretend to care for votes before immediately pivoting to border crackdowns.

•	Pairs well with **Deportation Crackers**, dry and crumbling under pressure.

•	Serve with **Migrant Wage Vinaigrette**, a dressing made entirely of underpaid labor with no benefits.

Warning:
May cause frustration, displacement, and the realization that America's economy depends on immigrants it refuses to respect. Side effects include xenophobic rhetoric, detention centers filled with families, and CEOs claiming, "Americans just don't want these jobs." If symptoms persist, remember: the system was designed this way.

Woke Watercress and Citrus Salad

A bright, refreshing dish condemned by reactionaries who fear anything green, vibrant, or remotely nutritious. Packed with bold flavors and progressive ingredients, but guaranteed to enrage those who think seasoning is "woke indoctrination."

Serves: Millennials, Gen Z, and anyone who believes in basic human rights
Prep Time: A lifetime of listening to bad-faith arguments against equality
Cook Time: None, because systemic change shouldn't have to wait

Ingredients:

• 3 cups fresh watercress (as bitter as conservative think pieces on diversity)

• 1 grapefruit, peeled and segmented (pink, juicy, and constantly accused of having an agenda)

• 1 orange, peeled and sliced (bright, hopeful, and completely misrepresented by cable news)

• ½ small red onion, thinly sliced (for the tears shed over bad-faith culture wars)

• ¼ cup toasted almonds (because every progressive policy gets roasted by Fox News)

• 2 tablespoons olive oil (as smooth as a well-crafted protest chant)

• 1 tablespoon lemon juice (for that sharp, necessary bite of reality)

• 1 teaspoon honey (because even in opposition, kindness wins)

• ½ teaspoon salt (for the conservatives who say "stay salty" but can't handle the heat)

• ¼ teaspoon black pepper (mild, just like the majority of their outrage)

Instructions:

1. **Build a Solid Foundation:** Arrange the watercress in a large bowl, because real change starts with deep roots.

2. **Add the Layers of Progress:** Top with grapefruit, orange slices, and red onion, creating a mix of flavors as diverse as an inclusive society.

3. **Drizzle with Nuance:** Whisk together olive oil, lemon juice, honey, salt, and pepper, because seasoning, like intersectionality, is essential.

4. **Finish with a Crunch:** Sprinkle toasted almonds over the top for extra bite, much like every well-informed response to reactionary nonsense.

Serving Suggestions:

*   Best enjoyed at a **Diversity and Inclusion Brunch**, where people actually read books before banning them.

*   Pairs well with **Cancel Culture Crostini**, a snack that conservatives cry about while using it to build their careers.

*   Serve with a glass of **Equality Espresso**, a strong drink that wakes you up to the reality of systemic oppression.

Warning:
May cause outrage among people who don't understand the definition of "woke." Side effects include critical thinking, cultural awareness, and being accused of trying to "destroy Western civilization" for simply acknowledging history. If symptoms persist, continue educating yourself, and enjoy the salad.

Blame Game Beet and Goat Cheese Salad

A deeply red dish, tossed in deflection and finger-pointing, where every ingredient gets blamed for the mess but never the ones responsible. Drizzled with a dressing of gaslighting and served on a platter of pure bad faith.

Serves: Pundits, failed politicians, and anyone who refuses to take accountability
Prep Time: However long it takes to redirect responsibility
Cook Time: None, because it's always someone else's fault

Ingredients:

- 3 medium beets, roasted and sliced (red like the faces of those deflecting blame)

- ½ small red onion, thinly sliced (representing the layers of excuses peeled back over time)

- ½ cup crumbled goat cheese (soft, like every excuse made for corporate greed)

- ¼ cup toasted walnuts (because this endless blame cycle is nuts)

- 3 cups mixed greens (to create the illusion of balance)

- 2 tablespoons olive oil (for greasing the wheels of misinformation)

- 1 tablespoon balsamic vinegar (aged in decades of passing the buck)

- 1 teaspoon honey (a touch of sweetness to make the lies go down easier)

- ½ teaspoon salt (for the working class, told to "work harder")

- ¼ teaspoon black pepper (because mild outrage is all most people muster)

Instructions:

1.   **Prepare the Distractions:** Roast beets at 400°F for 40 minutes, much like politicians waiting out a scandal. Let cool, then slice into rounds that look eerily like targets.

2.   **Toss in False Narratives:** Combine mixed greens, beets, and red onion in a bowl, ensuring that no ingredient takes responsibility for the mess.

3.   **Dress with Misdirection:** Whisk together olive oil, balsamic vinegar, honey, salt, and pepper, much like a PR team crafting a statement that says nothing.

4.   **Finish with Empty Promises:** Sprinkle goat cheese and toasted walnuts over the top, making it appear richer than it really is.

5.   **Serve Cold, Like a Political Deflection:** Plate and enjoy, though expect to be told it's actually your fault for not liking it enough.

Serving Suggestions:

•   Best enjoyed at a **Corporate Layoff Luncheon**, where CEOs blame "economic downturns" while cashing bonuses.

•   Pairs well with **Whataboutism Wheat Crackers**, baked to shift focus elsewhere.

•   Serve with **Deflection Dressing**, a slippery mix that ensures no one takes responsibility.

Warning:
May cause frustration, loss of faith in leadership, and increased reliance on independent journalism. Side effects include endless political spin, misplaced outrage, and billionaires insisting the economy collapsed because "people just don't want to work." If symptoms persist, try eating the rich instead.

PUBLIC
SERVICES

Section 4: Main Courses of Misery

Main courses are meant to sustain us, but in a system built on tyranny, they become monuments to inequity. These winter dishes are overcooked policies served with a side of despair.

Recipes:

Infrastructure Lasagna

Education Reform Eggplant Parmesan

Military-Industrial Pot Roast

Climate Catastrophe Casserole

Stock Market Roullet Grilled Fish Steaks

The wealthy do not just want to own everything; they want to make sure no one else has a chance to own anything. This is why wages have been suppressed for decades while the cost of living skyrockets. This is why public goods, education, healthcare, housing, are privatized and turned into profit machines. This is why organized labor is crushed, why small businesses are swallowed by monopolies, why debt is weaponized as a form of modern servitude. The Supreme Court has ruled over and over again in favor of corporate power, ensuring that the few can exploit the many without consequence. These main courses are the bloated, grotesque symbols of excess that define a system built on inequality, a system where millions struggle while a handful of oligarchs hoard more wealth than they could ever spend.

Infrastructure Lasagna

A once-strong, layered foundation now crumbling under decades of neglect, corporate greed, and political grandstanding. Originally built to support the people, now held together by patchwork repairs, empty promises, and the occasional collapse.

Serves: Lobbyists, corrupt contractors, and politicians who keep kicking the can down the crumbling road
Prep Time: Decades of deferred maintenance and bad policy
Cook Time: Until a bridge collapses or an election cycle demands action

Ingredients:

- 12 lasagna noodles (cracked and barely holding together, like America's roads and bridges)

- 2 cups ricotta cheese (smooth, like every politician's infrastructure promises)

- 1 cup shredded mozzarella (for the illusion of stability)

- ½ cup grated parmesan (aged, much like our outdated water systems)

- 1 pound ground beef, or plant-based alternative (symbolizing the labor force, overworked and underpaid)

- 1 small onion, diced (for the many layers of bureaucratic red tape)

- 2 cloves garlic, minced (to mask the stench of mismanagement)

- 1 can (28 oz) crushed tomatoes (drained, like the public funds that were supposed to fix this mess)

- 2 tablespoons tomato paste (a concentrated version of corporate handouts)

- 1 teaspoon salt (not enough to preserve what's left)

- ½ teaspoon black pepper (for the small kick of outrage every time an overpass collapses)

- $\frac{1}{2}$ teaspoon red pepper flakes (a mild heat, like the public's simmering frustration)

- 1 teaspoon dried oregano (a nostalgic reminder of when the government actually funded infrastructure)

- 1 tablespoon olive oil (greasing the pockets of private contractors)

Instructions:

1. **Boil the False Promises:** Cook lasagna noodles according to package instructions, ensuring they remain structurally unsound, much like the nation's highways. Drain and set aside.

2. **Sauté the Mismanagement:** In a large pan, heat olive oil over medium heat. Add onion and garlic, cooking until fragrant, about the time it takes for a politician to announce yet another "bold new plan" with no real funding.

3. **Cook the Workforce into the Ground:** Add ground beef, cooking until browned. Stir in crushed tomatoes, tomato paste, salt, pepper, and red pepper flakes. Simmer for 15 minutes, allowing corporate contractors to overcharge for bare-minimum results.

4. **Construct the Layers of Neglect:** In a greased baking dish, start with a layer of noodles, followed by a thin layer of ricotta, a portion of the meat sauce, and a sprinkle of mozzarella. Repeat, stacking layer upon layer, just like bureaucratic delays and endless budget cuts.

5. **Top with False Solutions:** Finish with parmesan and a final layer of cheese to create the illusion of a well-funded system. Cover with foil to conceal all the structural failures beneath.

6. **Bake Until It's Too Late:** Bake at 375°F for 35 minutes, uncovering in the last 10 minutes to let the facade crisp up.

Serving Suggestions:

- Best enjoyed during an **Election Year Infrastructure Week**, where nothing actually gets built.

- Pairs well with **Bridges to Nowhere Breadsticks**, long, thin, and ultimately useless.

- Serve with a glass of **Toll Road Red Wine**, a drink that costs too much but somehow never improves the commute.

Warning:
May cause frustration, massive traffic delays, and tax dollars disappearing into private pockets. Side effects include pothole-related car damage, collapsing overpasses, and politicians using crumbling roads as a photo op. If symptoms persist, demand real public investment, but expect to be told there's just no money for it, despite another corporate bailout passing with bipartisan support.

Education Reform Eggplant Parmesan

A dish with a strong foundation, repeatedly gutted and rebuilt to serve private interests rather than the people. Layers of potential suffocated under standardized testing, corporate influence, and budget cuts, baked until all critical thought is thoroughly melted away.

Serves: Charter school investors, corrupt politicians, and anyone profiting off a deliberately underfunded public education system
Prep Time: Decades of policy failures, privatization schemes, and student debt crises
Cook Time: As long as it takes for another generation to realize they've been scammed

Ingredients:

- 1 large eggplant, sliced (representing the core of public education, now sliced apart by charter schools and school choice grifts)

- 1 teaspoon salt (for the underpaid teachers who keep the system running)

- 1 cup flour (dry and lifeless, like an underfunded textbook)

- 2 eggs, beaten (scrambled, much like education priorities after every election cycle)

- 1 cup breadcrumbs (prepackaged reforms that offer no real improvement)

- 1 teaspoon dried oregano (a nostalgic reminder of when public education wasn't a for-profit scheme)

- ½ teaspoon black pepper (to season the countless political debates with no actual solutions)

- 2 tablespoons olive oil (greasing the wheels for billionaire-backed school privatization)

- 1 can (28 oz) crushed tomatoes (watered down, much like every "bold new plan" for reform)

- 1 tablespoon tomato paste (concentrated effort from underpaid educators)

- •	1 teaspoon sugar (to sweeten the bitter reality of standardized testing)

- •	2 cloves garlic, minced (because the system stinks)

- •	1 cup shredded mozzarella (stretched thin, like every public school budget)

- •	½ cup grated parmesan (aged, like tenured teachers fighting for basic resources)

- •	¼ cup fresh basil, chopped (a rare fresh idea, usually ignored in favor of corporate interests)

Instructions:

1.	**Prepare the Underfunded Base:** Sprinkle salt over the eggplant slices and let sit for 20 minutes, drawing out excess bitterness, though it won't remove the sting of underpaid teachers struggling to provide basic supplies.

2.	**Coat in Bureaucracy:** Dredge each slice in flour, dip in beaten eggs, and coat with breadcrumbs mixed with oregano and black pepper. These layers provide the illusion of structure, much like overcomplicated policies that do little to fix the system.

3.	**Fry in Privatization Oil:** Heat olive oil in a pan and fry each eggplant slice until golden brown, about the time it takes for another billionaire to demand more school vouchers.

4.	**Simmer the False Promises:** In a saucepan, sauté garlic in a bit of olive oil, then stir in crushed tomatoes, tomato paste, and sugar. Simmer for 15 minutes, allowing lobbyists to add their own seasoning in the form of political donations.

5.	**Assemble the Failing System:** In a baking dish, layer sauce, fried eggplant, mozzarella, and parmesan, repeating until you've built an institution riddled with inefficiencies.

6.	**Bake Until Hope is Gone:** Cover with foil and bake at 375°F for 30 minutes, uncovering for the last 10 minutes so the cheese can form a crust, much like the hardened cynicism of overworked educators.

Serving Suggestions:

- Best enjoyed at a **Policy Summit Where No Teachers Are Invited.**

- Pairs well with **Standardized Testing Breadsticks**, a rigid, flavorless side that measures nothing of value.

- Serve with **Student Loan Red Wine**, aged in decades of interest and garnished with regret.

Warning:

May cause frustration, overcrowded classrooms, and the realization that billionaires have more say in education policy than teachers. Side effects include charter school grifts, massive student debt, and politicians insisting they "support teachers" while slashing their budgets. If symptoms persist, consider homeschooling, if they haven't made that illegal yet.

Military-Industrial Pot Roast

A slow-cooked, overfunded, and deeply entrenched dish, where the richest cuts go to defense contractors while the public is left with the scraps. Simmered for decades in endless conflict, inflated budgets, and bipartisan complicity, this roast feeds an empire built on war.

Serves: Defense lobbyists, war profiteers, and politicians who always find money for bombs but never for healthcare

Prep Time: As long as it takes for the next manufactured conflict to justify another trillion-dollar spending bill

Cook Time: Forever, because war is America's most profitable business

Ingredients:

- 3 pounds beef chuck roast (as tough and overextended as U.S. foreign policy)

- 2 tablespoons olive oil (for greasing the pockets of weapons manufacturers)

- 1 large onion, chopped (for the layers of secrecy in government contracts)

- 3 cloves garlic, minced (to mask the stench of war crimes)

- 4 cups beef broth (funded by taxpayer dollars, whether they like it or not)

- ½ cup red wine (because every arms dealer toasts to another year of record profits)

- 2 tablespoons tomato paste (concentrated, much like military propaganda)

- 3 large carrots, chopped (for the soldiers sent off to fight wars they didn't start)

- 2 potatoes, cubed (representing the veterans discarded after their service is no longer profitable)

- 1 teaspoon salt (not enough to preserve government accountability)

- •	½ teaspoon black pepper (a mild kick, like the media's questioning of war budgets)

- •	2 bay leaves (because no matter how long it cooks, we never learn from history)

- •	1 teaspoon smoked paprika (for the illusion of moral justification)

- •	1 teaspoon dried thyme (because America's been stuck in this cycle for too damn long)

Instructions:

1.	**Sear the Imperial Ambitions:** Heat olive oil in a large pot and sear the roast on all sides until golden brown, just enough to look respectable on the world stage while still destabilizing entire regions.

2.	**Sauté the Lies:** Add onion and garlic, cooking until softened, much like public resistance to yet another military budget increase.

3.	**Deglaze with War Profiteering:** Pour in red wine and scrape up the browned bits, ensuring every contractor gets a piece of the action.

4.	**Drown in Overspending:** Stir in beef broth, tomato paste, salt, pepper, paprika, and bay leaves. Bring to a simmer and let it stew in its own corruption.

5.	**Add the Human Cost:** Toss in carrots and potatoes, then cover and cook on low heat for 4-5 hours, long enough for another generation to be sent to war for corporate interests.

6.	**Serve with Manufactured Consent:** Remove bay leaves, slice, and plate, reminding diners that this dish will be served again next year, and the year after that.

Serving Suggestions:

- Best enjoyed at a **Bipartisan Defense Spending Gala**, where both sides agree war is good business.

- Pairs well with **Pentagon Pork Belly**, a dish that always expands, no matter the budget crisis.

- Serve with **Contractor Cornbread**, a side that absorbs as much funding as possible without ever fully delivering.

Warning:
May cause endless conflict, massive debt, and the belief that war is the only industry America truly excels at. Side effects include record-breaking defense budgets, declining public services, and veterans left to fend for themselves while CEOs rake in billions. If symptoms persist, demand cuts to military spending, but expect to be called unpatriotic.

Climate Catastrophe Casserole

A bubbling, overcooked disaster, packed with ignored warnings, corporate greed, and a slow-roasting planet. Smothered in greenwashing sauce and baked until irreversible, this dish ensures that the only thing left for future generations is the bitter taste of inaction.

Serves: Oil executives, billionaire space colonizers, and politicians who cash fossil fuel checks while pretending to care
Prep Time: Centuries of industrial pollution and political denial
Cook Time: Until the last ice cap melts

Ingredients:

- 2 cups crumbled environmental regulations (shredded for corporate convenience)

- 1 pound ground beef or plant-based alternative (representing the working class, cooked under extreme heat)

- 1 large onion, diced (for the many layers of ignored climate reports)

- 2 cloves garlic, minced (to mask the stench of corporate lobbying)

- 1 cup canned corn (because soon, fresh produce won't be an option)

- 1 can (15 oz) black beans, drained (the only thing left standing after another wildfire season)

- 1 teaspoon smoked paprika (to mimic the taste of a permanently scorched Earth)

- ½ teaspoon black pepper (for the mild inconvenience rich people feel when asked to change)

- ½ teaspoon cayenne (a small taste of the rising global temperature)

- 1 can (28 oz) diced tomatoes (watered down, just like every climate summit's final resolution)

- 2 tablespoons tomato paste (because fossil fuel companies keep doubling down)

- 1 cup shredded cheese (melting, much like the glaciers)

- 1 bag corn chips, crushed (because billionaires will be just fine, crunching over the ruins)

Instructions:

1. **Preheat to the Point of No Return:** Set your oven to 375°F, though soon, thanks to deregulation, this will be the average outdoor temperature.

2. **Sauté the Fossil Fuel Lies:** In a large pan, cook the onion and garlic until fragrant, like the promises of green energy that never materialize.

3. **Brown the Warnings:** Add ground beef or plant-based alternative and cook until browned, much like the air quality in cities choked by wildfire smoke.

4. **Drown in Greenwashing Sauce:** Stir in diced tomatoes, tomato paste, black beans, corn, smoked paprika, black pepper, and cayenne. Simmer for 10 minutes, long enough for another oil pipeline to be approved.

5. **Layer in Complacency:** Pour the mixture into a casserole dish, spreading it evenly before topping with shredded cheese and crushed corn chips, because, like politicians, it's all about the surface appearance.

6. **Bake Until It's Too Late:** Cover with foil and bake for 25 minutes, uncovering for the last 10 to let everything bubble over, much like the increasing number of climate disasters.

Serving Suggestions:

- Best enjoyed at a **Corporate Climate Pledge Dinner**, where executives sip champagne and promise to "reduce emissions by 2050."

- Pairs well with **Microplastic Martini**, a drink already inside you whether you like it or not.

- Serve with **Trickle-Down Tap Water**, a beverage that's either undrinkable or privatized, depending on where you live.

Warning:
May cause rising sea levels, mass extinction, and billionaires booking space flights while telling the rest of us to recycle more. Side effects include heatwaves, hurricanes, and politicians who pretend they don't own stock in oil companies. If symptoms persist, demand action, but expect to be told it's your fault for using a plastic straw.

Stock Market Roulette Grilled Fish Steaks

A high-risk, high-reward dish where the stakes are as unpredictable as Wall Street. Will you end up with a perfectly grilled bite of prosperity or a dry, overcooked collapse? Like the stock market, this meal is all about timing, luck, and knowing when to pull the plug before everything burns.

Serves: Those watching their savings disappear
Prep Time: The time it takes for a bubble to inflate
Cook Time: As fast as a financial crash when billionaires pull out first

Ingredients:

- 2 fresh tuna or halibut steaks (high-quality, because only the rich get bailouts)

- 2 tablespoons olive oil (liquid gold, like a golden parachute)

- 1 teaspoon sea salt (not to be confused with investor tears)

- ½ teaspoon black pepper (like the daily uncertainty of your 401(k))

- 1 teaspoon smoked paprika (a deep burn, like your retirement fund)

- 1 teaspoon garlic powder (sharp, like another economic downturn)

- ½ teaspoon cayenne pepper (optional, for those who like their risks spicy)

- Juice of 1 lemon (because every dip in the market is an "opportunity")

- 1 tablespoon soy sauce (depth, like billionaire portfolios always seem to have)

- 1 teaspoon honey (a touch of sweetness, like trickle-down promises)

- 1 tablespoon fresh parsley (a green garnish, unlike your account balance)

Instructions:

1.   **Market Speculation:** Pat fish dry and season with salt, pepper, paprika, garlic, and cayenne, layering on risk like a hedge fund stacking assets.

2.   **Inflate the Bubble:** In a bowl, mix olive oil, lemon juice, soy sauce, and honey. This is your marinade, the illusion of security before the inevitable downturn.

3.   **Invest and Hope:** Marinate fish for 15-20 minutes. Any longer, and the acid will break it down, just like deregulation eventually collapses the economy.

4.   **Grill at Your Own Risk:** Heat a grill or pan over medium-high. Sear for 3-4 minutes per side. Pull too soon, it's undercooked; wait too long, it's dry and worthless.

5.   **Pull Out Before the Crash:** Remove when just cooked through but still tender. Rest for a couple of minutes, timing is everything in finance and food.

6.   **Serve with Economic Anxiety:** Garnish with parsley and an extra squeeze of lemon, then check your stock portfolio, if you dare.

Serving Suggestions:

•   Best paired with **Gerrymandered Gumbo**, because nothing says cooked books like cooked seafood.

•   Pairs well with **Tanking Market Scalloped Potatoes**, a side dish that shrinks unpredictably before it reaches your plate.

•   Serve with **Overleveraged Red or White Wine**, a bold vintage with strong notes of regret.

Warning:
May cause regret and the realization that no matter how well you plan, the wealthiest will always cash out first. If symptoms persist, consider diversifying, or just stop gambling in a system designed for you to lose.

PROSPERITY

Section 5: Desserts of Despair

Desserts should bring joy, but in the land of tyranny, they are saccharine illusions. These confections are seasonal distractions that leave a bitter aftertaste of inequity.

Recipes:

Tiered Tyranny Cake

Tariff Tax Toffee Pudding

American Dream Gingerbread House

Inequality Ice Cream Cake

Holiday Hypocrisy Cookies

The wealthy do not just want to own everything; they want to make sure no one else has a chance to own anything. This is why wages have been suppressed for decades while the cost of living skyrockets. This is why public goods, education, healthcare, housing, are privatized and turned into profit machines. This is why organized labor is crushed, why small businesses are swallowed by monopolies, why debt is weaponized as a form of modern servitude. The Supreme Court has ruled over and over again in favor of corporate power, ensuring that the few can exploit the many without consequence. These main courses are the bloated, grotesque symbols of excess that define a system built on inequality, a system where millions struggle while a handful of oligarchs hoard more wealth than they could ever spend.

Tiered Tyranny Cake

A dessert stacked with inequality, sugar-coated lies, and a foundation as shaky as late-stage capitalism. The rich feast on the top, and the rest fight for crumbs.

Serves: The masses, but only if they fight for a slice
Prep Time: Centuries of hoarded wealth and stolen labor
Bake Time: As long as the ruling class can keep the illusion going

Ingredients:

Bottom Tier (The Working Class – Overworked & Underpaid):

- 1 ½ cups all-purpose flour (bleached, like history books)

- 1 cup sugar (taxed higher than billionaire wealth)

- ½ teaspoon salt (like wages, barely enough to matter)

- 1 teaspoon baking powder (false promises of mobility)

- ½ cup milk (watered down, like corporate benefits)

- ½ cup oil (subsidized, because the government picks winners)

- 2 eggs (free-range, unlike workers in dead-end jobs)

Middle Tier (The Shrinking Middle Class – Squeezed & Stagnant):

- 1 ½ cups cake flour (fancier, but struggling)

- ¾ cup sugar (shrinking like retirement funds)

- ½ teaspoon salt (because the system still stings)

- ½ cup sour cream (soured, like the American dream)

- ½ cup butter (melting under pressure)

- 2 eggs (scrambled, like your 401(k) after a crash)

Top Tier (The Elite – Light, Airy, Untouched by Consequence):

- 1 cup almond flour (imported and exclusive)

- ¾ cup powdered sugar (privileged and untaxed)

- ¼ teaspoon salt (a suggestion, like regulations for the rich)

- ½ cup heavy cream (full-fat indulgence, like their tax breaks)

- ½ cup butter (golden, like their parachutes)

- 1 egg (hand-selected, like their justices)

Frosting (Propaganda & Performative Generosity):

- 2 cups butter (enough fat for the fat cats themselves)

- 4 cups powdered sugar (sweet lies about economics)

- 1 teaspoon vanilla (a false promise of shared prosperity)

- ¼ cup milk (just enough to pretend they care)

Instructions:

1. **Bake the Inequality:** Prepare each cake layer separately. Bake at 350°F for 25 minutes, checking frequently, unlike tax audits for the rich.

2. **Cool While the Public Struggles:** Let cakes cool completely. The longer you wait, the worse things get, unless you're at the top.

3. **Stack the System:** Place the dense, overworked bottom layer first, followed by the struggling middle, and finally the delicate, untouchable top.

4. **Frost with Lies:** Spread buttercream evenly, masking injustice with sweet deception.

5. **Serve Unequally:** Slice generously for the top, modestly for the middle, and let the rest fight for crumbs.

Final Thought:
Eat before it collapses, like unchecked greed, this structure won't last.

Tariff Tax Toffee Pudding

A dense, sticky dessert that ensures the working class gets trapped in economic policy they had no say in, while corporations pass the costs onto consumers. Sweetened with deception, soaked in inflation, and served with a side of political gaslighting.

Serves: Billionaire trade negotiators, corporate monopolies, and politicians who claim tariffs "help the economy" while raising prices for everyone else

Prep Time: Decades of trade wars and corporate loopholes

Cook Time: Until the working class realizes they're the only ones paying

Ingredients:

- 1 cup pitted dates, chopped (representing the expired promises that tariffs would help the economy)

- ¾ cup boiling water (heated to the breaking point, like consumer frustration)

- 1 teaspoon baking soda (because much like trade policies, this dish is full of hot air)

- ½ cup unsalted butter, softened (greasing the hands of corporate lobbyists)

- ¾ cup brown sugar (dark and sticky, just like hidden tariffs buried in fine print)

- 2 eggs (beaten down, like small businesses crushed by import taxes)

- 1 teaspoon vanilla extract (the illusion of a well-balanced system)

- 1 ¼ cups all-purpose flour (representing the working class, stretched thin)

- 1 teaspoon baking powder (because, unlike wages, this dish actually rises)

Toffee Sauce:

- 1 cup heavy cream (rich, like the top 1% profiting from economic manipulation)

- ½ cup unsalted butter (melting, much like the public's purchasing power)

- ½ cup brown sugar (a sickly-sweet distraction from inflation)

- 1 tablespoon dark rum (because you'll need a drink after reading your grocery bill)

- Pinch of salt (to taste, since price hikes have already salted the wound)

Instructions:

1. **Soften the Blow:** In a bowl, pour boiling water over the chopped dates, stir in baking soda, and let sit for 10 minutes, just enough time for another think tank to argue tariffs "boost domestic growth" while wages remain stagnant.

2. **Whisk the Working Class:** In another bowl, beat butter and brown sugar until light and fluffy, much like the promises that tariffs would rebuild American industry. Add eggs and vanilla, then mix in the flour and baking powder.

3. **Blend the Economic Burden:** Stir in the softened date mixture, folding everything together, ensuring the working class is fully incorporated into paying for corporate greed.

4. **Bake Until Profits Peak:** Pour batter into a greased baking dish and bake at 350°F for 30-35 minutes, or until a toothpick inserted in the center comes out clean, just like billionaires avoiding taxes.

5. **Drown in Rising Costs:** While baking, make the toffee sauce by combining heavy cream, butter, brown sugar, and rum in a saucepan. Simmer until thick, much like the concentration of wealth in the hands of the few.

6. **Serve Hot, Just Like Inflation:** Poke holes in the baked pudding and pour the toffee sauce over the top, letting it absorb like corporate price hikes disguised as "supply chain issues."

Serving Suggestions:

- Best enjoyed at a **Chamber of Commerce Banquet**, where executives justify outsourcing while sipping $500 wine.

- Pairs well with **Economic Austerity Ice Cream**, a flavorless, bare-minimum accompaniment that costs extra.

- Serve with **Consumer Debt Coffee**, brewed from the bitter reality of skyrocketing prices.

Warning:
May cause financial instability, mass layoffs, and corporate CEOs pretending to care about the middle class. Side effects include rising grocery costs, manipulated trade deals, and politicians gaslighting workers into believing these policies help them. If symptoms persist, just remember: billionaires aren't paying these tariffs, you are.

American Dream Gingerbread House

A beautifully decorated façade with a crumbling foundation, built on borrowed time and bad mortgages. Sweet on the surface, but structurally unsound, much like the illusion of upward mobility in modern America. Guaranteed to collapse under the weight of economic reality.

Serves: Banks, real estate speculators, and anyone who still believes in trickle-down economics
Prep Time: Generations of propaganda about hard work and success
Cook Time: Until the next financial crisis wipes out homeownership for the working class

Ingredients:

- 3 ½ cups all-purpose flour (representing the working class, constantly stretched to hold everything together)

- 1 tablespoon ground ginger (a spice as sharp as the housing market crash)

- 2 teaspoons cinnamon (warming, much like the false security of a 30-year mortgage)

- ½ teaspoon salt (because the American Dream has always been seasoned with struggle)

- 1 teaspoon baking soda (a rising agent, much like home prices outpacing wages)

- ½ cup unsalted butter, softened (to grease the pockets of the mortgage industry)

- ½ cup brown sugar (dark and sticky, like adjustable-rate mortgage contracts)

- 1 large egg (beaten down, much like renters trying to buy their first home)

- ½ cup molasses (slow-moving, like the ever-elusive promise of affordable housing)

- 1 teaspoon vanilla extract (an artificial sense of security)

Royal Icing (The Illusion of Stability):

- 3 cups powdered sugar (for the pristine, picture-perfect exterior)

- 2 egg whites (whipped into a frenzy, like the 2008 housing bubble)

- ½ teaspoon cream of tartar (to add just enough structure before everything comes crashing down)

Instructions:

1. **Mix the Ingredients of Disillusionment:** In a bowl, whisk together flour, ginger, cinnamon, salt, and baking soda, because every system needs a solid foundation, even if this one is built on predatory lending.

2. **Cream the Corporate Greed:** In another bowl, beat butter and brown sugar until fluffy, much like the promises of homeownership as a path to security. Add egg, molasses, and vanilla, stirring well.

3. **Roll Out the Redlining:** Combine the wet and dry ingredients, kneading the dough into something that resembles stability, until you realize the foundation is cracking.

4. **Bake the Dream to a Crisp:** Roll out dough, cut into house-shaped pieces, and bake at 350°F for 12-15 minutes, or until edges are firm, unlike real housing policies, which favor speculation over people.

5. **Assemble with Empty Promises:** Use royal icing to hold the walls together, applying it liberally, like government bailouts for banks while homeowners are left to foreclose.

6. **Decorate with Sugar-Coated Lies:** Pipe icing along the roof and windows, covering up structural weaknesses with colorful distractions, just like real estate ads selling unaffordable homes to millennials drowning in debt.

Serving Suggestions:

- Best enjoyed at a **Banker's Holiday Party**, where they toast to record profits while evictions spike.

- Pairs well with **Foreclosure Fudge**, a bittersweet dessert made from financial ruin.

- Serve with **Gentrification Ginger Tea**, a hot beverage that drives longtime residents out of their own neighborhoods.

Warning:
May cause housing insecurity, rising rent, and extreme frustration at the fact that a gingerbread house is more affordable than an actual home. Side effects include predatory loans, the increasing privatization of housing, and billionaires buying up entire neighborhoods while telling you to "just stop eating avocado toast." If symptoms persist, demand rent control and affordable housing, though expect resistance from the same people flipping the properties.

Inequality Ice Cream Cake

A dessert with multiple layers, some rich, indulgent, and overflowing with excess, while others are paper-thin and barely holding together. Frozen solid at the top, melting into a mess at the bottom, much like America's wealth distribution.

Serves: Billionaires, trust fund heirs, and corporate executives who claim "hard work" got them where they are
Prep Time: Centuries of systemic exploitation
Cook Time: Indefinite, because wealth hoarding ensures nothing ever trickles down

Ingredients:

- 2 pints premium vanilla ice cream (representing the top 1%, untouched by struggle)

- 2 pints generic, off-brand ice cream (for the working class, forced to stretch every dollar)

- 1 sheet of dense chocolate cake (a solid foundation, much like the working poor propping up the elite)

- ½ cup crushed cookies (crumbled, like every promise of upward mobility)

- 1 cup whipped cream (light and fluffy, like trickle-down economics)

- ¼ cup gold sprinkles (because wealth is always on display at the top)

- ½ teaspoon sea salt (for the tears of the underpaid and overworked)

- 1 tablespoon dark rum (a splash of reality, best served with a side of despair)

Instructions:

1. **Build the Wealth Gap:** Let premium ice cream soften slightly and spread it in an even layer on a baking sheet lined with parchment. Freeze until firm, ensuring those at the top stay comfortably frozen in their wealth.

2. **Prepare the Struggle Layer:** Spread the off-brand ice cream in a thinner layer beneath the premium one, barely covering the base, much like wages that haven't kept up with inflation. Freeze again.

3. **Assemble the Exploitation:** Place the dense chocolate cake at the very bottom, compressing the entire structure, just like an economic system that ensures the rich rest on the backs of workers.

4. **Crumble the Dreams:** Sprinkle crushed cookies over the top, because while wealth at the top grows exponentially, those at the bottom are left with nothing but crumbs.

5. **Top with Empty Promises:** Spread a generous layer of whipped cream over everything, a light, airy illusion that hides the harsh reality beneath.

6. **Decorate with Greed:** Scatter gold sprinkles on the top, ensuring that the wealthiest layer gets all the sparkle while everyone else gets nothing.

7. **Freeze Until the Bottom Melts Away:** Return to the freezer until fully set, though expect the lower layers to soften and collapse while the top remains perfectly intact.

Serving Suggestions:

- Best enjoyed at a **Billionaire Birthday Bash**, where the cake is cut but never shared fairly.

- Pairs well with **Overtime Espresso Shots**, a bitter drink consumed by those working multiple jobs just to afford rent.

- Serve with **Lobbyist Liquor**, aged in tax breaks and served neat to the political elite.

Warning:
May cause increased resentment, stagnating wages, and an ever-growing gap between the ultra-rich and everyone else. Side effects include record corporate profits while working-class families struggle, billionaires launching vanity space flights, and CEOs telling you that "no one wants to work anymore." If symptoms persist, demand progressive taxation and workers' rights, but be prepared for a flood of think pieces calling you a radical.

Holiday Hypocrisy Cookies

A classic seasonal treat, sugar-coated on the outside but filled with the bitter aftertaste of performative generosity and empty platitudes. Served at corporate holiday parties where executives preach "family values" while slashing paid leave and gutting benefits.

Serves: Fortune 500 CEOs, politicians who cut social programs while quoting scripture, and anyone who weaponizes "the spirit of giving" for PR

Prep Time: However long it takes for corporations to craft their holiday-themed press releases

Cook Time: Until the charitable façade crumbles

Ingredients:

- 2 ½ cups all-purpose flour (bleached of any real substance, like corporate holiday charity drives)

- 1 teaspoon baking soda (a small rise, much like wages, just enough to claim progress but not enough to matter)

- ½ teaspoon salt (for the workers clocking in on Christmas while their bosses vacation)

- 1 cup unsalted butter, softened (greased with corporate bonuses)

- 1 cup granulated sugar (sweet, but artificially so, like a politician's "thoughts and prayers")

- ½ cup brown sugar (darker and more complex, like the truth behind every PR stunt)

- 2 eggs (beaten down, like the workforce during peak holiday season)

- 2 teaspoons vanilla extract (a hint of warmth, quickly overshadowed by exploitation)

- 1 teaspoon cinnamon (a seasonal distraction from the realities of economic inequality)

- ½ teaspoon nutmeg (spicy, like the debates over whether billionaires should exist)

98

- ½ cup red and green sprinkles (to make it look festive, even when it's hollow inside)

Instructions:

1. **Preheat the Performative Generosity:** Set your oven to 350°F, just warm enough to give the illusion of holiday warmth, but not enough to actually provide comfort.

2. **Cream the Contradictions:** Beat butter, granulated sugar, and brown sugar together until light and fluffy, much like corporate statements about "giving back" while union-busting.

3. **Whisk in the Guilt-Free Messaging:** Add eggs and vanilla, blending until smooth, ensuring all problematic policies are well-disguised.

4. **Mix in the Seasonal Misdirection:** In a separate bowl, whisk together flour, baking soda, salt, cinnamon, and nutmeg. Slowly incorporate into the wet ingredients, forming a dough as dense as tax loopholes for the ultra-rich.

5. **Roll in PR Spin:** Form into balls, then coat in red and green sprinkles, because nothing says "holiday spirit" like empty gestures that distract from exploitation.

6. **Bake Until the Illusion is Set:** Place on a baking sheet and bake for 10-12 minutes, or until the edges are just crisp enough to pass as sincere.

7. **Cool and Serve with a Side of Gaslighting:** Let cool before serving at a workplace potluck where everyone is told to "think of the company as family."

Serving Suggestions:

- Best enjoyed at a **Corporate Holiday Party**, where your Christmas bonus is an expired Starbucks gift card.

- Pairs well with **Mistletoe Minimum Wage Cocoa**, a warm drink that somehow still leaves you cold.

- Serve with **Trickle-Down Eggnog**, a rich, frothy beverage that never actually reaches the people at the bottom.

Warning:
May cause frustration, performative philanthropy, and the realization that corporate charity is just another tax write-off. Side effects include sudden rage at billionaires donating a fraction of their wealth while workers rely on food banks, CEOs making heartfelt speeches while outsourcing jobs, and politicians using "Christian values" to justify cutting social services. If symptoms persist, consider organizing a strike, but don't be surprised when management claims they can't afford to pay you more right after announcing record profits.

Message in a Bottle –
Drinking and Smoking Your Dessert

Not everyone ends a meal with a slice of cake or a plate of cookies. Some people prefer their sugar in a glass, their comfort in a bottle, their indulgence in smoke curling from the tip of something rolled just right. Dessert isn't always something you chew, it's something you sip, something you inhale, something that lingers longer than a bite of pie ever could. Maybe it's a nightcap, maybe it's a stiff pour of reality, maybe it's just the ritual of ending something sweet with something strong. Maybe it's an old-fashioned poured neat, a drag of something illicit, a quiet rebellion wrapped in a stemmed glass or flickering at the end of a cigarette.

Call it liquid courage, call it a moment of indulgence, call it a rebellion against a system that wants you to stay sharp, stay productive, stay under control. Because the truth is, sometimes the best way to end a meal is to raise a glass to the absurdity of it all. To take a drag and exhale the weight of another day spent fighting against forces that never seem to crack. To let the burn of whiskey remind you that you're still here, still standing, still defiant. Maybe dessert isn't about sugar. Maybe it's about savoring the fire. Maybe it's about embracing the moments of reckless joy, of stolen pleasure, of tasting something that isn't manufactured scarcity or corporate greed. Maybe it's about reminding yourself that you can still take what's yours, one slow sip or inhale at a time.

Sláinte!

Bonus Section: Entertaining at the End of Empathy

In the harsh winter of tyranny, table manners matter, especially when you're dining with those who profit from systemic oppression. These tips will help you survive the banquet of inequity with dignity, or at least a stiff drink.

Recipes:

Denial Eggnog

Gaslighter Hot Toddy

Apathy Aperol Spritz (Winter Edition)

Coup Cocoa

Whataboutism Mulled Wine

For decades, we have been told that politeness is a virtue, that civility is the cornerstone of democracy. But civility means nothing when it is wielded as a weapon to silence opposition. The same billionaires who gut social programs and crush workers then have the audacity to demand respect at the dinner table. They steal trillions and call it capitalism. They fund think tanks to dismantle civil rights and call it free speech. They rig the courts and call it democracy. These drinks and hosting tips are for those who refuse to play along, who refuse to shake hands with the people who are robbing them blind.

Denial Eggnog

A rich, frothy holiday drink spiked with willful ignorance and sweetened with empty reassurances. Best enjoyed by those who insist everything is fine while the world crumbles around them.

Serves: Climate change deniers, corporate CEOs, and politicians who think thoughts and prayers are a policy solution
Prep Time: Decades of avoiding reality
Cook Time: None, because the consequences will come whether they acknowledge them or not

Ingredients:

- 4 large egg yolks (separated, much like the wealthy from the consequences of their actions)

- ½ cup granulated sugar (to mask the bitter truth)

- 2 cups whole milk (rich and creamy, like the lies fed to the public)

- 1 cup heavy cream (because the top 1% always gets the thickest cut)

- ½ teaspoon vanilla extract (a sweet distraction from real issues)

- ½ teaspoon ground nutmeg (warm and comforting, like the illusion that everything is under control)

- ¼ teaspoon ground cinnamon (a sprinkle of nostalgia for the good old days that never really existed)

- ¾ cup bourbon, rum, or brandy (because nothing helps you ignore reality like a stiff drink)

- Whipped cream, for topping (a fluffy layer of denial to cover what's beneath)

Instructions:

1. **Whisk the Excuses:** In a large bowl, whisk together egg yolks and sugar until smooth, much like a politician dodging a difficult question.

2.   **Heat the False Reassurances:** In a saucepan over medium heat, warm the milk, heavy cream, vanilla, nutmeg, and cinnamon, stirring constantly, just enough to keep the illusion from breaking.

3.   **Temper the Lies:** Slowly whisk the warm mixture into the egg yolks, ensuring they don't curdle, because nothing ruins a perfectly good deception like actual consequences.

4.   **Spike with Avoidance:** Stir in the liquor of choice, numbing the drinker just enough to ignore skyrocketing costs, environmental collapse, and the erosion of rights.

5.   **Chill Until Reality Sets In:** Let cool, then refrigerate for at least an hour, because it's easier to pretend problems don't exist when they're served cold.

6.   **Top with a Fluffy Cover-Up:** Pour into glasses and finish with whipped cream, ensuring the drink is as insulated from the truth as a billionaire's bunker.

Serving Suggestions:

•   Best enjoyed at a **Corporate Holiday Party**, where executives praise their record profits while laying off workers.

•   Pairs well with **Holiday Hypocrisy Cookies**, for the full empty gesture experience.

•   Serve with a side of **Trickle-Down Toast**, which promises much but delivers nothing.

Warning:

May cause delayed reactions to crises, misplaced optimism, and the persistent belief that "everything will work itself out." Side effects include extreme apathy, cognitive dissonance, and billionaires telling you to "just stay positive" while hoarding resources. If symptoms persist, shake yourself awake, take action, and maybe spike your next drink with a little revolution instead.

Gaslighter Hot Toddy

A warm, soothing drink designed to convince you that your suffering isn't real, your anger is misplaced, and everything is actually just fine. Sweetened with manipulation and served piping hot to make you second-guess your own reality.

Serves: Gaslighting politicians, corporate bosses, and anyone who insists "it's not that bad" while standing in front of a five-alarm fire
Prep Time: Just long enough for you to doubt yourself
Cook Time: Until you start believing the lies

Ingredients:

- 1 cup boiling water (for the slow burn of manufactured doubt)

- 1 black tea bag (steeped in bad-faith arguments)

- 2 tablespoons honey (overly sweetened to make the lies go down easier)

- 1 tablespoon fresh lemon juice (for the sharp sting of being told your experience isn't real)

- ½ teaspoon grated ginger (subtly spicy, like the feeling that something's off but you can't quite prove it)

- ¼ teaspoon cinnamon (for the warmth of false reassurances)

- 2 ounces whiskey or bourbon (because sometimes you need something strong to stomach the gaslighting)

- 1 lemon slice, for garnish (a bright distraction from the actual problem)

- 1 cinnamon stick, for stirring (because the narrative is always being spun)

Instructions:

1. **Steep in Doubt:** Pour boiling water over the black tea bag and let it steep for 3-5 minutes, giving the misinformation enough time to take hold.

2. **Sweeten with Manipulation:** Stir in honey, ensuring the false reassurances coat everything evenly.

3.   **Add a Twist of Deflection:** Squeeze in the fresh lemon juice, because nothing redirects accountability like a little acidic misdirection.

4.   **Spike with Intention:** Pour in whiskey or bourbon, because gaslighting is always more effective when it dulls your senses.

5.   **Garnish with Distraction:** Add a lemon slice and a cinnamon stick, giving it the perfect polished look to make you forget what's actually happening.

6.   **Serve Hot and Unquestioned:** Sip slowly while someone tells you that your concerns are overblown, you're imagining things, or "it's always been this way."

Serving Suggestions:

•   Best enjoyed at a **Political Press Conference**, where accountability is avoided at all costs.

•   Pairs well with **Both Sides Brussels Sprout Salad**, a dish that insists everyone is equally at fault.

•   Serve with **Denial Eggnog**, because nothing pairs better with gaslighting than complete avoidance.

Warning:
May cause self-doubt, misplaced guilt, and the creeping suspicion that you're the problem when you're not. Side effects include frustration, exhaustion, and billionaires insisting that everything is "just the free market at work." If symptoms persist, take a deep breath, trust your instincts, and throw the whole drink in the fire.

Apathy Aperol Spritz (Winter Edition)

A cold, bitter cocktail designed to lull you into complacency while the world burns around you. Lightly effervescent, deceptively cheerful, and just strong enough to keep you detached from reality, this drink ensures you stay comfortably numb through another season of manufactured despair.

Serves: Politicians who "strongly condemn" injustice but do nothing, voters who have given up, and billionaires who sip from insulated towers while telling you to "just work harder"

Prep Time: A lifetime of learned helplessness

Cook Time: None, because inaction is the key ingredient

Ingredients:

- 2 ounces Aperol (bright and bitter, like the first flicker of outrage before it fades)

- 3 ounces prosecco (bubbly and distracting, like empty platitudes)

- 1 ounce cranberry juice (seasonal, yet sour, much like every broken promise)

- 1 ounce club soda (diluted, just like every policy meant to "help" the people)

- ½ teaspoon maple syrup (a false touch of warmth, masking the underlying indifference)

- 1 rosemary sprig, for garnish (a decorative nod to better times that never quite arrive)

- 1 orange slice, for garnish (a bright distraction from growing inequality)

Instructions:

1. **Fill a Glass with Misdirection:** Add ice to a wine glass, ensuring the drink stays cold, much like political enthusiasm in a midterm election year.

2. **Pour in the Resignation:** Add Aperol, prosecco, and cranberry juice, stirring lightly so as not to disturb the illusion that things will get better on their own.

3. **Dilute with Indifference:** Top with club soda, ensuring the strength of the drink, and the strength of any real movement, becomes watered down.

4. **Sweeten with False Hope:** Stir in a touch of maple syrup, because even the worst systems need a little sugarcoating to keep people from revolting.

5. **Garnish with Performative Concern:** Add a rosemary sprig and an orange slice, making the drink appear thoughtful and full-bodied when, in reality, it's as empty as a politician's speech.

6. **Serve with a Shrug:** Sip slowly while telling yourself that "nothing ever changes anyway."

Serving Suggestions:

• Best enjoyed at a **Moderate Voter Cocktail Hour**, where everyone agrees things are bad but refuses to demand real change.

• Pairs well with **Gerrymandered Gumbo**, a dish that ensures nothing ever moves forward.

• Serve with **Denial Eggnog**, the perfect companion for ignoring uncomfortable truths.

Warning:
May cause resignation, political disengagement, and an increased reliance on alcohol to tolerate the news. Side effects include doomscrolling, avoiding hard conversations, and billionaires thriving while insisting there's "nothing we can do." If symptoms persist, put down the drink, get mad, and start organizing.

Coup Cocoa

A deceptively sweet, frothy drink with an undercurrent of authoritarian bitterness. Starts off smooth and comforting but quickly turns dark and overwhelming, leaving an aftertaste of sedition and regret. Best enjoyed by those who cry about democracy while actively dismantling it.

Serves: Wannabe dictators, corporate-funded extremists, and politicians who lose elections but refuse to accept reality
Prep Time: Years of eroded democratic norms
Cook Time: Just long enough for a mob to storm the Capitol

Ingredients:

- 2 cups whole milk (rich, like the donors funding insurrectionist campaigns)

- ½ cup heavy cream (thick, like the skulls of coup supporters ignoring the Constitution)

- ½ cup dark chocolate, chopped (bitter, like the realization that democracy is fragile)

- 2 tablespoons cocoa powder (for the deep, dark undercurrent of authoritarian ambitions)

- 2 tablespoons sugar (a spoonful of propaganda to help the lies go down)

- 1 teaspoon cinnamon (warm, like the glow of burning democratic institutions)

- ½ teaspoon cayenne pepper (for the inevitable, violent escalation)

- 1 teaspoon vanilla extract (to disguise the bitter truth)

- 2 ounces spiced rum or bourbon (because coups always go better with a little liquid courage)

- Whipped cream, for topping (a fluffy illusion of legitimacy)

- Grated nutmeg, for garnish (a final touch of nostalgia for the republic that once was)

Instructions:

1.   **Simmer the Conspiracy Theories:** In a saucepan over medium heat, warm the milk, heavy cream, cocoa powder, sugar, cinnamon, and cayenne pepper. Stir continuously, ensuring misinformation spreads evenly.

2.   **Melt the Electoral Process:** Add chopped dark chocolate and stir until smooth, much like a well-executed disinformation campaign.

3.   **Spike with Sedition:** Stir in vanilla extract and liquor of choice, making the drink stronger, because bad ideas always go down easier when you're drunk.

4.   **Garnish with Denial:** Pour into mugs and top with whipped cream, ensuring the surface looks soft and harmless while the chaos simmers beneath.

5.   **Finish with Nostalgia:** Sprinkle with grated nutmeg, a decorative nod to a democracy that used to function before billionaires and right-wing media got involved.

Serving Suggestions:

•   Best enjoyed at a **Post-Election "Audit" Party**, where votes are only valid if your side wins.

•   Pairs well with **Gerrymandered Gumbo**, a dish that ensures the right people stay in power no matter the vote count.

•   Serve with **Both Sides Brussels Sprout Salad**, a side that insists democracy's downfall is just a matter of perspective.

Warning:
May cause authoritarian creep, mass radicalization, and a deeply uncomfortable realization that democracy depends on people actually defending it. Side effects include violent mobs, sham investigations, and billionaires funding think tanks that justify it all. If symptoms persist, put down the cocoa, read a history book, and start taking threats to democracy seriously.

Whataboutism Mulled Wine

A hot, spiced distraction technique served in a steaming cup of deflection. Each sip swirls with rich, historical grievances, irrelevant comparisons, and a heavy pour of misdirection, ensuring no real accountability ever takes place.

Serves: Bad-faith debaters, corrupt politicians, and anyone whose go-to argument is "But what about…?"
Prep Time: However long it takes to dodge the real issue
Cook Time: Just enough to cloud the conversation

Ingredients:

- 1 bottle of red wine (aged in centuries of false equivalencies)

- ½ cup brandy (strong enough to blur the lines between facts and nonsense)

- 1 orange, sliced (bright, like the topic you were actually discussing before the derailment)

- 2 tablespoons honey (for the overly sweet, condescending tone of every whataboutist)

- 2 cinnamon sticks (for stirring the conversation away from the point)

- 5 whole cloves (to punctuate every dishonest argument)

- 3 star anise pods (to add complexity, even where none actually exists)

- ½ teaspoon black peppercorns (for the small bite of misplaced outrage)

- 1 teaspoon grated ginger (subtle but sharp, like the shift from meaningful discussion to rhetorical nonsense)

Instructions:

1. **Heat the Distraction:** In a large saucepan over medium-low heat, combine red wine, brandy, and honey, stirring gently, like someone slowly guiding a conversation off-course.

2. **Layer in the False Comparisons:** Add orange slices, cinnamon sticks, cloves, star anise, peppercorns, and ginger. Let

everything infuse, much like bad arguments seeping into public discourse.

3.   **Simmer in Bad Faith:** Bring to a gentle heat, careful not to boil, just like how whataboutism is best served warm, never hot enough to face real scrutiny.

4.   **Strain Out the Substance:** Remove from heat, strain out the spices, and pour into mugs, ensuring the final product is smooth, polished, and completely devoid of meaningful content.

5.   **Garnish with Deflection:** Serve with an orange slice and a cinnamon stick, adding the illusion of thoughtfulness to an otherwise empty discussion.

Serving Suggestions:

•   Best enjoyed at a **Congressional Ethics Hearing**, where no one answers direct questions.

•   Pairs well with **Both Sides Brussels Sprout Salad**, a dish that insists accountability is unfair.

•   Serve with **Denial Eggnog**, for those who refuse to believe a problem exists at all.

Warning:
May cause circular arguments, loss of productive conversation, and complete avoidance of real solutions. Side effects include politicians dodging questions, Twitter debates going nowhere, and billionaires funding think tanks that say oppression is subjective. If symptoms persist, demand a direct answer, but don't expect to get one.

Bonus Bonus: Feast for a Crowd
The Elimination of Social Security

The measure of a society is how it treats its most vulnerable. By that standard, we have failed. They have turned retirement into a privilege, old age into a punishment, and dignity into a commodity. Social Security was a promise, one they intend to break for profit.

Recipe:

Privatized Pension Pig Roast & Trickle-Down Marinade:
A whole pig stuffed with IOUs, slow-roasted over a pit of generational theft. Serves an ever-shrinking crowd of wealthy elites while the rest are left gnawing on scraps.

For a Small but Angry Crowd
Crony Capitalism Leg of Lamb:
A leg of lamb rubbed with privilege, slow-roasted in deregulation, and basted with public funds that never reach the table. Serves an elite inner circle while everyone else fights over the dry, overcooked ends.

If there's one thing the ruling class hates more than paying workers, it's letting them retire. Social Security wasn't a gift; it was won by a labor movement that knew capitalism would exploit people until their last breath. The manufactured "crisis" is just another excuse to gut it, just like they defunded schools, housing, and healthcare. The wealthy hoard trillions while claiming we "can't afford" the program workers paid into for decades. The goal is clear: keep people working until they die. And when they finally dismantle it, leaving millions in poverty, they'll demand civility. They'll call it reform. We know it's theft.

Privatized Pension Pig Roast

A slow-roasted feast for the ultra-wealthy, packed with broken promises and basted in corporate greed. Carefully engineered to serve only the top 1%, while the rest are left licking the empty bones.

Serves: The hedge fund class, private equity CEOs, and politicians who never had to work a real job
Prep Time: 40 years of payroll taxes, drained and mismanaged
Cook Time: Until the last pension disappears into a private retirement account that only benefits Wall Street

Ingredients:

- **1 whole pig** (representing Social Security, promised to the people but now reallocated for corporate use)

- **3 cups dry-rubbed false reassurances** ("Don't worry, Social Security will be there when you retire!")

- **1 dozen shredded pension plans** (ripped apart by corporate raiders and underfunded by decades of tax breaks for billionaires)

- **2 cups hedge fund stock drippings** (extracted from workers' retirement accounts and funneled into executive bonuses)

- **¼ cup trickle-down marinade** (so thin it disappears before reaching the middle class)

- **4 cloves garlic, minced** (because this whole thing stinks)

- **3 tablespoons salt** (to season the bitter reality of working until death)

- **2 teaspoons black pepper** (like politicians' reassurances, it adds some heat but no real substance)

- **1 tablespoon smoked paprika** (for that artificially charred "we care" effect)

- **1 cup taxpayer-funded subsidies** (invisible to the public, but absolutely essential for feeding Wall Street)

- **1 stick butter, melted** (because in the end, everything just greases the pockets of the rich)

- **A handful of crushed retirement savings** (for garnish, discarded before serving)

Instructions:

1. **Prepare the Pig:** Pat the pig dry, ensuring any excess funds meant for retirees are fully absorbed into hedge fund accounts before roasting. Using a sharp knife, carve deep pockets into the meat and stuff with shredded pension plans, these will disintegrate almost immediately, leaving nothing but an empty promise of financial security.

2. **Rub with False Reassurances:** In a small bowl, mix salt, pepper, paprika, and minced garlic. Massage this blend into the pig, much like politicians massage the truth when they tell you Social Security will still be there in 30 years. Let sit at room temperature while the corporate class finds new ways to gut entitlement programs.

3. **Baste in Trickle-Down Marinade:** Heat a saucepan over medium heat and combine the melted butter with hedge fund stock drippings and trickle-down marinade. Stir well, though no matter how much you mix, it will always favor the wealthiest portion of the dish.

4. **Roast Over the Fire of Deregulation:** Preheat your oven to 300°F (the same temperature as Wall Street lobbyists' efforts to undermine worker protections). Place the pig in a roasting pan and slowly cook for 6-8 hours, occasionally basting with taxpayer-funded subsidies. The slower the roast, the more time billionaires have to extract wealth before the system collapses.

5. **Carve with Precision:** Once fully cooked, carve into generous portions for executives and hedge fund managers, leaving only the toughest, least nutritious scraps for the remaining 99%. Garnish with crushed retirement savings, which should be tossed aside before serving.

6. **Serve with a Side of Indifference:** Best enjoyed with a smug sense of superiority while telling underpaid workers they should have just saved more.

Serving Suggestions:

- Pair with **Austerity Applesauce**, a bitter reduction of wages and rising inflation.

- Serve with **401(k) Kale Slaw**, a dish that looks promising but ultimately leaves you unsatisfied.

- Best enjoyed at an exclusive think tank dinner, where the only discussion about Social Security is how to dismantle it further.

Warning:
This dish is not suitable for those who expected to retire with dignity. Side effects include rising poverty rates among the elderly, mass disillusionment with capitalism, and the grim realization that you worked your entire life only to be told there's nothing left for you. If you experience financial ruin, do not contact your government representatives, they are currently enjoying their lifetime pensions, fully funded by the taxes you paid.

Trickle-Down Marinade

A thin, flavorless sauce that never quite reaches the bottom of the dish. Best enjoyed by the wealthy, while everyone else is left dry.

Serves: Billionaires and corporate executives (working people should not expect a taste)
Prep Time: 40 years of failed economic policy
Cook Time: None, it evaporates before real change happens

Ingredients:

- ½ cup olive oil (greasy, like corporate tax loopholes)

- ¼ cup stock market drippings (extracted from underpaid labor)

- 2 tablespoons Dijon mustard (because it sounds fancy, but changes nothing)

- 1 tablespoon honey (a spoonful of sugar to sell the scam)

- 2 teaspoons apple cider vinegar (soured over decades of economic inequality)

- 1 teaspoon salt (not enough to preserve public benefits)

- ½ teaspoon black pepper (just for show, like most political promises)

- ½ teaspoon crushed red pepper flakes (symbolizing the anger of the working class)

Instructions:

1. In a small bowl, whisk together all ingredients until fully combined, much like politicians blend corporate interests into economic policy.

2. Let sit for several decades, ensuring wealth pools at the top while the bottom remains dry.

3. Use sparingly, this marinade is designed to coat the richest cuts, leaving nothing for the rest.

Serving Suggestions:

- Best drizzled over **Privatized Pension Pig Roast**, ensuring the ultra-wealthy remain well-fed.

- Pairs well with **Austerity Brussels Sprouts**, a dish that never quite satisfies.

- Serve at elite fundraisers where the term "working class" is used as an abstract concept.

Warning:
Despite decades of promises, this marinade has never actually benefited the majority. Side effects include rising income inequality, gutted social programs, and billionaires telling you to "just work harder."

Spicy Crony Capitalism Leg of Lamb

A fire-roasted cut of influence, coated in backroom deals, and slow-cooked in public subsidies. The heat is reserved for the working class, while the elite enjoy the juiciest portions, untouched by consequence.

Serves: Billionaire donors, think tank economists, and politicians who claim the market is "self-correcting" as they rig it in their favor
Prep Time: Decades of deregulation, monopolization, and corporate handouts
Cook Time: As long as it takes for another tax loophole to pass

Ingredients:

- 1 bone-in leg of lamb (a premium cut, just like corporate tax breaks)

- ¼ cup olive oil (greasing the right hands)

- 4 cloves garlic, minced (essential for covering up the stench of corruption)

- 2 tablespoons Dijon mustard (sharp, like insider trading tips)

- 1 tablespoon honey (sweet, like the lies sold to the public)

- 1 tablespoon fresh rosemary, chopped (reserved for the privileged few)

- 1 tablespoon fresh thyme, chopped (aged, like outdated economic theories still in practice)

- 2 teaspoons salt (rationed out like fair wages)

- 1 teaspoon black pepper (for the small kick of public outrage)

- 1 tablespoon smoked paprika (because everything about this system is cooked)

- 1 teaspoon cayenne pepper (a burning reminder of who really pays the price)

- 1 teaspoon crushed red pepper flakes (scattered, like workers left behind by automation)

- 1 cup red wine (a luxury only the top earners get to enjoy)

• 1 cup beef or lamb stock (funded entirely by the taxpayers)

Instructions:

1. **Prepare the Pay-to-Play Rub:** In a bowl, mix olive oil, garlic, mustard, honey, rosemary, thyme, salt, black pepper, paprika, cayenne, and red pepper flakes. This fiery blend ensures those at the bottom feel the heat while the top remains well-insulated.

2. **Coat in Wealth Protection:** Rub the spice mixture generously over the lamb, concentrating the best seasoning at the top. Let sit at room temperature for 30 minutes, long enough for another industry bailout to pass.

3. **Sear the Profits:** In a large roasting pan, heat oil over high heat and sear the lamb on all sides until browned, much like regulatory agencies that only step in after the damage is done.

4. **Bake in Lobbyist Influence:** Pour the red wine and stock into the pan, ensuring a rich, complex sauce that mysteriously evaporates before reaching the table. Cover loosely with foil and roast at 325°F for 2.5 to 3 hours, basting occasionally to keep the top moist while the bottom dries out.

5. **Carve Up the Economy:** Remove from the oven and let rest for 15 minutes before slicing. Serve the most tender, flavorful cuts to executives while reminding the rest that "if they just worked harder," they'd have better portions.

6. **Serve with a Side of Deflection:** Spoon the reduced sauce over the lamb, though most of it has already disappeared into offshore accounts.

Serving Suggestions:

• Best enjoyed at a **Super PAC Fundraiser**, where money buys access but not accountability.

• Pairs well with **Inflation-Adjusted Flatbread**, which somehow costs more every year for less flavor.

• Serve with **Regressive Tax Reduction Sauce**, a rich topping that only benefits those who don't need it.

Warning:
May cause record-breaking CEO bonuses, worker layoffs, and the slow erosion of economic stability. Side effects include increased cost of living, mass wealth hoarding, and a small group of billionaires insisting this is just how capitalism is supposed to work. If symptoms persist, consider roasting the billionaires instead.

A Recipe, or 3, for Prosperity

The winter kitchen of tyranny is one of exploitation and greed. But every recipe can be rewritten, every dish reimagined.

The billionaires who have plundered the world, hoarded resources, and crushed the working class under their boots expect not just obedience but gratitude. They demand we admire their grotesque excess, celebrate their manufactured success, and show deference to their ill-gotten wealth. They buy politicians, gut regulations, steal wages, and then have the audacity to call it "entrepreneurship." They rig the system in their favor, then mock the rest of us for not being able to climb a ladder they pulled up decades ago. And when we protest? When we dare to suggest that maybe this obscene wealth hoarding is a crime against humanity? They cry victim. They whimper about class warfare, cancel culture, and the unfairness of being held accountable. They expect table manners as they devour the last scraps of the American Dream.

But we owe them nothing, no respect, no civility, no compromise. We owe them only their extinction from public life, their wealth redistributed, their influence shattered. Ban billionaires? No. Braise them. They are not geniuses, job creators, or innovators. They are parasites, feeding off the labor of others while convincing the world they deserve their status. Every trillion hoarded is a trillion stolen, every loophole exploited is another worker left behind. The only recipe worth following now is one that removes them from power completely. The future is not built on their generosity, because they have none. It is built on reclaiming what they stole and ensuring no one ever hoards this much wealth again. The era of billionaire dominance must be burned to the ground. From those ashes, we will cook something better.

Post-Capitalism Prosperity Chicken

A rich, nourishing dish for the world we deserve, one where workers are valued, communities thrive, and no one is left to starve while billionaires hoard the feast. This recipe celebrates the death of unchecked greed and the rise of something better: collective abundance, shared prosperity, and a meal where everyone gets a plate. And don't worry, this chicken is bird flu-free, just like a society free from corporate greed is free from manufactured crises and preventable disasters.

Serves: Everyone, because in a just world, no one goes hungry
Prep Time: The time it takes to dismantle economic inequality
Cook Time: Faster than a billionaire can stash their wealth offshore

Ingredients:

- 2 large boneless, skinless chicken breasts (raised ethically, because exploitation has no place at this table)

- 1 teaspoon salt (seasoned with fair wages)

- ½ teaspoon black pepper (for a little bite, because justice requires boldness)

- 1 teaspoon smoked paprika (a warm reminder that the old system is going up in flames)

- 2 tablespoons olive oil (cold-pressed by worker-owned cooperatives)

- 1 tablespoon fresh lemon juice (zesty, like the energy of economic revolution)

- 2 cloves garlic, minced (because truth should always be strong and fragrant)

- 1 teaspoon honey (a touch of sweetness, because life post-capitalism is better for everyone)

- ½ teaspoon red pepper flakes (for a kick, because change should be exciting)

- ¼ cup fresh parsley, chopped (green like sustainable policies and debt-free futures)

Instructions:

1.   **Liberate the Chicken:** Place the chicken breasts on a cutting board and flatten slightly, ensuring even cooking, just like a fair economy ensures equal opportunity.

2.   **Marinate in Justice:** In a bowl, mix olive oil, lemon juice, garlic, honey, and spices. Let the chicken soak in this flavorful revolution for at least 30 minutes, because good things take time, but they're worth it.

3.   **Cook with Collective Strength:** Heat a pan over medium-high heat and sear the chicken until golden brown on each side, about 5-6 minutes per side. The heat of change is necessary, it transforms what was once raw potential into something nourishing.

4.   **Let it Rest, but Not Too Long:** Remove from heat and let sit for a few minutes, because even after revolution, the people must gather their strength before rebuilding.

5.   **Garnish with a Future Worth Fighting For:** Sprinkle with fresh parsley and serve with your favorite sides, ideally something fresh and vibrant, because abundance is meant to be shared.

Serving Suggestions:

•   Best enjoyed while toasting to universal healthcare, living wages, and a world without billionaires.

•   Pairs well with **Infrastructure Lasagna**, a layered dish that proves investment in the people is always the right move.

•   Serve with **Workers' Wine**, because those who build the world deserve to celebrate it.

Warning:
Side effects may include radical hope, dismantling wealth hoarding, and realizing that a better world isn't just possible, it's necessary. If symptoms persist, redistribute the meal and keep building the future.

Tiramisu for Triumph

A dessert of defiance, layered with resilience and dusted with revolution. Unlike tyranny, which crumbles under pressure, this tiramisu stands strong, built on the foundation of community, shared power, and the sweet taste of justice. This is not just a dessert; it's a celebration of everything we refuse to let go of: joy, abundance, and a future where we all rise together.

Serves: A table where everyone gets a seat
Prep Time: The time it takes to overthrow oppression
Chill Time: Just enough for the movement to take hold

Ingredients:

- 1 ½ cups strong brewed espresso (bold and awakening, like collective action)

- 3 tablespoons dark rum or amaretto (a little fire, because victory is worth toasting)

- 8 ounces mascarpone cheese (smooth, like a well-executed general strike)

- 1 cup heavy cream (rich, but shared, because in a just world, indulgence is for everyone)

- 3 egg yolks (beaten like the forces of oppression)

- ½ cup sugar (sweet, like a world where billionaires are history)

- 1 teaspoon vanilla extract (pure, like the taste of liberation)

- 24 ladyfingers (standing together, because solidarity is the key to survival)

- 2 tablespoons cocoa powder (dark, deep, and powerful, like the roots of resistance)

- Shaved dark chocolate for garnish (because the revolution is bittersweet, but always worth it)

Instructions:

1.   **Brew the Awakening:** Mix the espresso with the rum or amaretto, letting the bitterness remind you that complacency is not an option.

2.   **Whip Up the Resistance:** In a bowl, beat together the egg yolks, sugar, and vanilla until thick and pale, proof that a little agitation creates strength.

3.   **Layer the Revolution:** In a separate bowl, whip the heavy cream until soft peaks form, then fold in the mascarpone until smooth and unified, just like a people's movement.

4.   **Soak Up the Change:** Briefly dip each ladyfinger into the espresso mixture, quick but decisive, like the action needed to dismantle systems of oppression. Lay them in a single layer in a dish, forming the foundation of your victory.

5.   **Build the Future:** Spread half the mascarpone mixture over the soaked ladyfingers, then repeat with another layer. This is the work of rebuilding, layer by layer, stronger each time.

6.   **Dust the Old World Away:** Finish with a generous dusting of cocoa powder, a reminder that oppression, once exposed, loses its power.

7.   **Chill, But Not for Too Long:** Refrigerate for at least 4 hours, because while movements take time to build, the best victories come when we act with urgency.

8.   **Serve with Defiance:** Garnish with shaved chocolate, slice generously, and share widely, because joy is meant to be collective, never hoarded.

Serving Suggestions:

•   Best enjoyed at **The People's Feast**, where wealth is shared and no one is left behind.

•   Pairs well with **Post-Capitalism Prosperity Chicken**, because justice tastes better when it's seasoned right.

•   Serve with **Workers' Wine**, and raise a glass to the future we are creating together.

Workers' Wine

A full-bodied beverage for those who keep the world running. A toast to the laborers, the organizers, the ones who build, grow, teach, and heal, without whom nothing would exist. Unlike the wealth hoarded by the ruling class, this drink is meant to be shared, poured generously, and enjoyed without exploitation.

Serves: Everyone who's ever been underpaid, overworked, and still kept going
Prep Time: The time it takes to recognize your worth
Drink Time: As long as the revolution takes

Ingredients:

- 1 bottle of bold red wine (deep, rich, and strong, just like the working class)

- ½ cup fresh orange juice (because solidarity is bright and refreshing)

- 2 tablespoons honey (sweet, like the victories of collective action)

- 1 cinnamon stick (warm, like the fire of the labor movement)

- 3 cloves (sharp, like the memory of every stolen wage and broken promise)

- ½ teaspoon nutmeg (for depth, because the fight for justice has layers)

- 1 small apple, thinly sliced (fruit of the labor that should belong to the workers, not the bosses)

- 1 small orange, thinly sliced (because zest is necessary for any uprising)

- ½ cup brandy (optional, but sometimes you need a little extra strength to face the system)

Instructions:

1. **Gather the People:** In a large pot, combine the wine, orange juice, honey, cinnamon, cloves, and nutmeg. Stir over low heat, letting the flavors merge like a well-organized strike.

2.   **Warm, Don't Burn:** Let the mixture heat slowly, never boil. Revolution is about patience and precision, not reckless destruction. Simmer for about 15 minutes, stirring occasionally.

3.   **Add the Fruits of Labor:** Drop in the sliced apple and orange, letting them soak up the warmth, just as workers lift each other up when the system tries to grind them down.

4.   **Pour with Purpose:** Ladle the drink into mugs or heatproof glasses. If using brandy, add a splash before serving, because sometimes, resistance needs an extra kick.

5.   **Raise a Glass and Take What's Yours:** Sip slowly, savoring every drop, because a world where workers are valued is one worth fighting for.

Serving Suggestions:

•   Best enjoyed while organizing, unionizing, and dismantling corporate greed.

•   Pairs well with **Post-Capitalism Prosperity Chicken**, a meal that proves there's more than enough for everyone.

•   Serve with **Mutual Aid Mashed Potatoes**, because feeding each other is the real trickle-down economics.

Final Thought:
Workers build the world, yet too often, they are left with nothing. This drink is a reminder that they deserve more, more rest, more pay, more respect, more joy. So raise your glass to labor, to resistance, to a future where the feast belongs to the people who made it possible. Sláinte to the workers. The world is ours.

List of Prints

1. *Power* — 8

2. *Yum* — 12

3. *Reform* — 34

4. *Greed* — 46

5. *Equality* — 58

6. *Public Services* — 70

7. *Prosperity* — 86

8. *Denial* — 102

9. *Security* — 114

10. *Soon* — 124

About EATMS Productions

What's happening to women now is not random. It's structural.

Policy, culture, technology, and power are moving in the same direction.

EATMS maps them clearly and shows how to respond.

This title is part of an ongoing body of work. All EATMS Productions titles, across all series, authors, and formats, are components of a single connected project.

Start here: EATMS System Primer — Free Bundle
https://eatms.gumroad.com/l/dyvzbw

For full catalog or inquiries: eatms.me

Free survival booklet + EATMS updates: email "EATMS" to eatms@pm.me

Please feel free to burn part or all of this book, safely, as an effigy.

www.ingramcontent.com/pod-product-compliance
Lightning Source LLC
Chambersburg PA
CBHW031234250726
48655CB00005B/1956